Reading Knowledge

For Jenny

Reading Knowledge

An Introduction to Barthes, Foucault, and Althusser

Michael Payne

BLACKWELL
Publishers

First published 1997

2 4 6 8 10 9 7 5 3 1

Blackwell Publishers Inc.
350 Main Street
Malden, MA 02148
USA

Blackwell Publishers Ltd
108 Cowley Road
Oxford OX4 1JF
UK

Library of Congress Cataloging in Publication Data
Payne, Michael.
Reading knowledge : an introduction to Barthes, Foucault, and
Althusser / Michael Payne.
p.   cm.
Includes bibliographical references and index.
ISBN 0-631-19566-1 (alk. paper).—ISBN 0-631-19567-X (pbk. : alk. paper)
1. Barthes, Roland—Contributions in criticism.   2. Foucault,
Michael—Contributions in criticism.   3. Althusser, Louis—Contributions
in criticism.   4. Criticism.   5. Knowledge, Theory of.   I. Title.
PN81.P38   1997
801'.95'0904—dc21
96-46163
CIP

British Library Cataloguing in Publication Data
A CIP catalogue record for this book is available from the British Library.

Typeset in 10.5 on 12.5 pt Garamond 3
by Best-set Typesetter Ltd., Hong Kong
Printed in Great Britain by
Hartnolls Ltd, Bodmin, Cornwall

This book is printed on acid-free paper

Contents

Preface

The aim of this book is to provide an introduction to the principal writings of Roland Barthes, Michael Foucault, and Louis Althusser by focusing in some detail on their common interest in the forms and conditions of knowledge. It is often falsely claimed in popular journalistic accounts of these writers that they abandoned any concern with truth, meaning, and value for the free play of language and theoretical speculation. A careful reading of their texts, on the contrary, reveals their profound commitment to a critical understanding of how truth, meaning, and value are constituted in language and in nonverbal texts. What Althusser said of Foucault holds true for all three of them: they were master teachers who taught how to read works of knowledge. While carefully investigating the mercurial semiotics of cultural forms, Barthes was relentlessly in search of a medium of signification that would render rather than displace the real. Foucault investigated the history of systems of thought in order to expose the power of knowledge and to examine the epistemes that are fundamental to the principal modes of thought that have come into prominence since the Renaissance. Finally, Althusser set out to read the classic texts of Marxism in a way analogous to Lacan's reading of Freud: to recover and to assess the radically innovative historical knowledge that Marx had begun to produce, which made it possible for him to begin to distinguish between ideology and the science of political economy.

Reading Knowledge is the second installment in a sequence of books that examine major texts of French critical and cultural theory. Like its predecessor. *Reading Theory: An Introduction to Lacan, Derrida, and Kristeva* (1993), *Reading Knowledge* is an exercise in theoretical criticism in the sense that its objects of investigation are theoretical texts, while its methods are those of literary criticism. Usually, when the texts examined here are difficult to read, it is because their arguments proceed metaphorically or their allusions to other texts are indirect or buried. The limited ambition of this book, then, is purposefully to blur the distinction that Thomas De Quincey made between the literature of knowledge and the literature of power and to read these investigations of the possibilities and limits of knowledge as rhetorically and conceptually invested in the powers of art.

Chapters 1 to 3 examine in considerable detail brief texts by Barthes, Foucault, and Althusser that seem to be their own strategically designed introductions to their major projects. Chapters 4 to 6 take up what I consider to be the most important books by each of these writers: Foucault's *The Order of Things*, Barthes's *S/Z*, and Althusser's *Reading Capital*. Here, rather than dealing with the micro-structures of the texts as in the earlier chapters, I have concentrated on larger textual components because the richness of detail in these books may cause readers to lose sight of their controlling arguments and their contributions to the theory of reading. Chapter 7 examines specific texts by Barthes, Althusser, and Foucault that deal with one of the visual arts in an effort to investigate the assumption that knowledge – whether as theory, enlightenment, vision, illumination, or insight – is in some sense visual. Chapter 8 briefly examines the work of Gilles Deleuze in the context provided by the earlier chapters.

I had originally intended to deal with Deleuze in much greater detail. His immensely challenging work, however, does not naturally lend itself to the procedure that I have followed with Barthes, Foucault, and Althusser, despite his close intellectual and personal connections with them. One reason it does not is that several brief texts by Deleuze in *Dialogues* and *Negotiations* could with equal justification be taken as his own introductions to his project. Furthermore, although *Anti-Oedipus* has been for some time his most widely read book, *What Is Philosophy?*, his final collaboration with Félix Guattari, may turn out to have a more lasting importance. Deleuze's two volumes on cinema, which are essential for an understanding of his thinking about visual imagery, presuppose an extensive knowledge of film theory and the ability to recall details in several hundred films, neither of which I possess. Once David Macey's forthcoming biography of Deleuze appears, it should be possible to assess his writing more systematically. My own sense is that Deleuze's critical investment in the history of philosophy provided him with a foundation for believing in the regenerative powers of philosophy in the face of the kinds of epistemological crisis that Barthes, Foucault, and Althusser also witnessed. For that reason – and in the hope that Deleuze's conviction that a non-repressive philosophical recovery from Marx, Nietzsche, and Freud is possible – I have concluded this book with a brief preliminary sketch of his work.

I plan to follow this study of Barthes, Foucault, and Althusser with a commentary on some major French feminist texts by Luce Irigaray, Hélène Cixous, Catherine Clément, Sarah Kofman, and Michèle Le Doeuff, who, because of economy of space, can be treated best together, although their feminist critiques work within the disciplines of philosophy and the creative arts.

In case my conviction about these writers gets lost in the details of the commentary to follow, I should point out here that in my judgment Barthes, Foucault, Althusser, and Deleuze have written about human subjectivity, language, social practice, and history in ways that are of inescapable importance for the humanities and social sciences during this twilight of the twentieth century. Although they have been well served by their translators, I have often cited passages from the French texts of their writings in support of observations about the poetics of their prose or details in their arguments. My own textual procedure is what the French call indirect free style, that is, I try to enter into the argumentative mode of these texts, while simultaneously explicating their rhetorical strategies, in order to deal both with argumentation and stylistic matters together. The amount of space I devote to a given text is not a veiled judgment of its importance but rather of its difficulty. When, on occasion, I find the text I comment on to be mistaken, I do not hesitate to say so. When there has been a controversy about one of these texts that has subsided, however, I refer to that in the notes.

My greatest debts are the most difficult to acknowledge as deeply as I feel them. My daughter Jenny Payne has been my ideal reader. She has talked with me at length about the issues discussed here and has been both consistently supportive and persistent with questions about the truth claims made both by her father and by the writers I discuss. I have also greatly benefited from the opportunities to present portions of this book in the form of lectures and seminars at Bucknell University and at Southern Oregon State College in Ashland, Oregon, where most of the book was written. I especially want to thank James Rice, Lynn Cazabon, Linden Lewis, Carol White, Tony Cieri, Emmanuel Eze, and Glynis Carr for their responses to some of my early reflections on Foucault in the course of the Knight seminars on cultural studies. On the occasion of the Magritte exhibition at the Hayward Gallery in London, Sir Frank Kermode shared with me his knowledge of surrealism in a way that has been most helpful. As a teacher of literature, I have been very fortunate in having worked with an extraordinarily gifted faculty in philosophy at Bucknell University. I owe a great personal and intellectual debt to Jeff Turner, Gary Steiner, and especially Richard Fleming. My colleagues Greg Clingham, Pauline Fletcher, John Murphy, and Harold Schweizer are also continual sources of friendship and intellectual stimulation. Unfortunately, at a time when library services are more and more computerized, it is seldom possible to know by name those who have been most helpful with research questions. But I greatly appreciate, nonetheless, the assistance I received from librarians at the British Library, the London Library, the Bertrand Library at Bucknell University, the Southern Oregon State College Library, and the library of the Warburg Institute at the University of London.

Finally, I wish to thank Andrew McNeillie of Blackwell Publishers, whose professional advice, sound judgment, and lasting friendship are invaluable to me. Sandra Raphael's sharp eyes and fine critical sense have once again saved me from several unfortunate errors, for which she has my sincere thanks.

Acknowledgements

I am grateful to the following publishers for permission to quote from the texts indicated:

Dialogues, by Gilles Deleuze and Claire Parnet, trans. Hugh Tomlinson and Barbara Habberjam (New York: Columbia University Press, 1987).
S/Z, by Roland Barthes, trans. Richard Miller (Oxford: Blackwell, 1990).
This Is Not a Pipe, by Michel Foucault, trans. James Harkness (Berkeley: University of California Press, 1982).

Abbreviations

CI   Karl Marx, *Capital*, volume I (London: Lawrence and Wishart, 1964).

CII   Karl Marx, *Capital*, volume II ed. Frederick Engels (London: Lawrence and Wishart, 1969).

F   Michael Foucault, "Nietzsche, Genealogy, History," in *Language Counter-Memory, Practice*, trans. Donald F. Bouchard (Ithaca, NY: Cornell University Press, 1977).

GI   Karl Marx and Frederick Engels, *The German Ideology* (London: Lawrence and Wishart, 1968).

MC   Michel Foucault, *Les Mots et les choses* (Paris: Gallimard, 1966).

N   Friedrich Nietzsche, *On the Genealogy of Morals and Ecce Homo*, trans. Walter Kaufmann and R.J. Hollingdale (New York: Vintage, 1967).

PT   Roland Barthes, *The Pleasure of the Text*, trans. Richard Miller (New York: Hill and Wang, 1975).

RB   Roland Barthes, *Roland Barthes*, trans. Richard Howard (Berkeley: University of California Press, 1994).

SE   *The Standard Edition of the Complete Psychological Works of Sigmund Freud*, trans. James Strachey (London: The Hogarth Press and The Institute of Psycho-Analysis, 1974), 24 vols.

SW   Karl Marx and Frederick Engels, *Selected Works in One Volume* (London: Lawrence and Wishart, 1968).

S/Z   Roland Barthes, *S/Z* (Paris: Editions du Seuil, 1970).

1

Barthes's "From Work to Text"

Roland Barthes, who will doubtless be remembered as one of the most important literary critics of the twentieth century, was also a pioneer in the field of semiotics and the most generously eclectic cultural theorist of his time. Constantly inventive and experimental, Barthes was truly an essayist in the sense that he wrote to weigh and to test ideas and simultaneously to put on trial his own methods of investigation and styles of writing. But because Barthes was systematically attentive to the ways language and other semiotic systems are embedded in culture – to the extent that they are also the means by which culture reflects upon and renews itself – the texts he produced are always subtly allusive. In at least two ways the metaphor of the pianist, which he often invoked to describe reading processes, also captures his project as a writer: First, he worked as a performer rather than a composer of ideas; and second, any individual performance of his captures only a single potentiality of an idea. It is not surprising, therefore, that he was determined to bring the roles of writer and reader, musician and listener as close together as possible. There is another important, if somewhat looser, similarity between Barthes's writing and musical performances. Although he readily admits that when language turns to interpret music, the results are usually unsatisfactory, there are nonetheless certain "limit works," as he calls them – such as Bach's *The Art of the Fugue* – which aspire to self-interpretation, as though they are music that is in search of both the limits and essence of music.[1] Barthes's own writing is of this sort. In his constant self-reflexivity, however, he manages also to be belletristic in the best sense, in that his is a style of criticism that is attentively and determinedly located within literary culture and manifests itself in prose of extraordinary refinement and delicacy.

Several features of Barthes's work, however, have contributed to the mistaken view that his project is hostile to art. For example, the title of his famous essay "The Death of the Author" has been cited as a rejection of human creativity, his studies in popular culture as an indication of an abandonment of aesthetic value, his efforts to extend linguistics to the structural analysis of narrative as an effort to undermine the humanities, his critical studies of images as a denigration of the imagination, and his contributions to semiotics as a betrayal of literature. Indeed, one of Barthes's most perceptive commentators has pointed out a parallel between Barthes and Rousseau as "hate-figures." The wholesale condemnation of their work "has nothing to do with truth and everything to do with ideological investments."[2] Like Foucault, Barthes wrote for both a popular and a professional readership. His thought and his reputation thus became subject to the vicissitudes of popular culture. For example, he was parodied in *French Without Tears*, a book that promised facetiously to teach its readers to speak "Roland-Barthes" in 18 easy lessons.[3] Because Barthes wrote prolifically without producing an obviously central book that is comparable, say, to Foucault's *The Order of Things* or Althusser's *Reading Capital*, it is difficult to study him systematically and to find the focal point of his work. In his essay "What Is Criticism?" he succinctly described the critic's job as the construction of "intelligibility for our time."[4] Barthes's commitment to this task is well illustrated in the best collection of his writing, Stephen Heath's *Music – Image – Text*, which includes the essay "From Work to Text," Barthes's most important critical manifesto.

First published in 1971, "From Work to Text" is also an extraordinarily economical statement of Barthes's synthesis of basic ideas in contemporary French literary theory. The stated purpose of the essay is to describe the change that took place in literary studies during the 1960s in relation to important innovations in such disciplines as linguistics, anthropology, Marxism, and psychoanalysis. Barthes's claim is neither that literary studies have simply submitted themselves to or been absorbed by these disciplines nor, necessarily, that they (along with those disciplines) have gone through any sort of definitive theoretical revolution. Rather, his claim is that a certain kind of interdisciplinarity has occurred as a result of a breakdown in the solidity of these disciplines and of literary criticism as well. What is unique about this interdisciplinarity born of epistemological crisis is that, rather than being an easily secure blend of already existing professional practices, this new thought is taking place violently within the established disciplines of the humanities and human sciences, where a new object of study and a new language are establishing a place for themselves. Barthes is reluctant to call this recent mutation an epistemological break. Like Althusser, Barthes sees the eruption of Marxism and Freudianism as the "real break" in Western thought, which in turn precipitated the crisis in the humanities and human sciences that is now so dramatically affecting the study of literature. He calls this mutation an "epistemological slide" (155). Although Barthes draws a rough comparison here with the movement from Newtonian to Einsteinian physics, in that now literary study demands that *"the relativity of the frames of reference* be included in the object studied" (156), recent changes in literary study amount to innovations quite distinct from paradigm shifts in the history of science. Barthes does not explicitly refer to Thomas Kuhn's model for understanding the structure of scientific revolutions – in which an established procedure for doing science (a paradigm) is exposed as no longer adequate and is therefore replaced by a new procedure (thus precipitating a scientific revolution)[5] – because his understanding of the recent crisis in literary criticism is that it is much messier and more disruptive than a Kuhnian paradigm shift, though less monumental than the epistemological break that resulted from the combined effects of Marxism, Freudianism, and structuralism.

The three changes in literary criticism that Barthes describes are (1) the relativization of the relation between the writer and the reader, which is largely the consequence of the new understanding of human beings that has resulted from the Marxist-Freudian epistemological break; (2) the designation of the *text* rather than the *work* as the object of literary study, which is the consequence both of the new understanding of human beings resulting from that epistemological break and of a new understanding of language and related nonverbal semiotic systems resulting from structuralism; (3) the production of a new language for the discipline of literary criticism that reflects the relativization of the frames of reference and the shift from work to text. Barthes proceeds to trace these changes through seven "propositions," which he offers as declarations or metaphorical "enunciations" rather than arguments. These propositions concern method, genres, signs, plurality, filiation, reading, and pleasure.

Method: The movement (or slide) from work to text is a consequence of a change in the method of literary study rather than the result of a concentration on, say, modern or avant-garde writing in opposition to classical literature. Unlike Sartre in *What Is Literature?* (1947) or later Kristeva in *Revolution in Poetic Language* (1974), Barthes does not neatly equate the text with the contemporary and the work with the classical. Indeed, Barthes's own writing includes major studies of the Bible, classical Greek drama, and Racine. To deal with a piece of literature as a work is to treat it as though it were a stable, physical object or "a fragment of substance" (156) that can be placed securely in a library or on a syllabus or that can be held in one's hands. To deal with a piece of literature as a text is to treat it as "a methodological field" and a "process of demonstration . . . in the movement of a discourse" (157). Whereas the text calls preconceived notions of genre, language, subjectivity, and reading into question, the work leaves them intact. This distinction also calls into question the nature of method itself. A text does not result merely from dealing with a work in a certain way, as though a piece of writing had simply submitted itself to any sort of reading. Rather, the text "knows itself as a text" (157) and thus demands that it be read a certain way. "The text is experienced only in an activity of production" that is on-going; it is not the product of a decisive "decomposition" (or deconstruction) of the work.

Genres: Just as the text is not the unique production of a certain historical moment, so also does it resist being contained in a hierarchy of value that would distinguish between what is good or serious and what is popular. A distinguishing feature of the text is its ability to exert a "subversive force" against what are presumed to be established generic classifications (such as novel, poem, essay) or disciplines (such as economics, philosophy, literature). Because the text is perpetually exploring the limits of such rules of enunciation as rationality and readability, it resists all forms of reductive classification. The text is *paradoxical* precisely in the sense that it calls any and all orthodoxy in question.

Signs: In his claim that "the text can be approached, experienced, in reaction to the sign" (158), Barthes is invoking an understanding of the relationship between the sign and the signified that is based on Saussure's *Course in General Linguistics* as it had been appropriated by Lacan and Derrida.[6] As though in an effort to stabilize and limit its meaning, the work closes in on a specific signified by the exercise of philology or hermeneutics. The work thus operates as a general sign that has been tamed, institutionalized, and civilized. The text, on the other hand, resists and subverts such efforts of closure by deferring the signified, taking the signifier instead as its field, in which a productive, dynamic looseness (or play) is maintained.[7] The text, therefore, resists regulating or comprehensive efforts to say what it means. It is metonymic and "radically symbolic." If the medium of the text is not language, it nevertheless is like language in that it is structured without center or close. Just as it calls the concept of method into question, so also does it lead to a critical investigation of the otherwise unexamined metaphoricality of structure, as Derrida had claimed.[8] Since, however, his critical investigation is also without closure and is subject to the same procedures it employs, Barthes resists, also like Derrida, the use of the mixed metaphor "poststructuralism."[9]

Plurality: In the first paragraph of his essay Barthes announces that his seven propositions are metaphorical (156). His account of the multiplicity of meaning in the text is therefore appropriately rich in imagery. The etymology of the word *text* implies that it is a tissue or woven fabric of meaning. Thus Barthes imagines the reader of the text approaching its cloth from a loose end. Alternatively, in an extended narrative image that he claims corresponds to his own situation when his vivid sense of the text came to him, it is as though the reader is strolling in a state of empty receptivity on the side of a valley, where an *oued* (or wadi) flows beneath him. Here the scene that Barthes imagines or recalls seems to be drawn from his stay in Morocco, where he had recently been teaching. What the reader (or stroller) perceives is a multiplicity of undifferentiated sensations that are "multiple, irreducible, coming from a disconnected, heterogeneous variety of substances and perspectives: lights, colours, vegetation, heat, air, slender explosions of noises, scant cries of birds, children's voices from over on the other side, passages, gestures, clothes of inhabitants near or far away" (159). In this extraordinarily sensuous account of textuality and reading, what is most important is that the details of the texts are initially experienced as incidents that are uncanny in their simultaneous familiarity and exotic strangeness. These textual incidents are half-identifiable in that their codes are known to the reader/stroller but their combination (or weave) is unique in the sense of being marked by difference rather than individuality. No universal grammar of the text is possible because the text is woven out of "citations, references, echoes, cultural languages which cut across and through it like a 'stereophony'" (160).

By declaring that there is "no 'grammar' of the text" (160), Barthes moves away from his earlier proposal for the structural analysis of narratives, which was based on his extension of the discoveries of transformational grammar concerning the syntax of sentences to account for the structure of narratives and other forms of discourse that exceed the sentence in length. That project was an elaboration of a specific understanding of the aim of structuralism which Barthes defined as the effort "to master the infinity of utterances [*paroles*] by describing the 'language' [*langue*] of which they are the products and from which they are generated" (80). Rather than searching for a central focus in the heterogeneity of language, as Saussure had done, Barthes in "From Work to Text" is attentive to the multiple citations, quotations, and other intertextual elements that are audible within a text. His persistent concern in both his earlier and later investigations, however, was to define the smallest constitutent units of the text in order to uncover its irreducible elements of meaning (88). Like the man possessed by demons in the Gospel of Mark (5:9), the text proclaims, "My name is Legion: for we are many." The text will therefore determinedly resist whatever monistic efforts – in the name of the church, Marxism, or other reductive hermeneutic – are exerted as reading strategies to curtail its multiple significations.

Filiation: One such effort to reduce polysemy is to posit various processes of filiation, as though the work were reducible in meaning to its sources. Three common processes of semiotic limitation have been the reduction of the work to a set of social and historical circumstances that are said to have produced it, to a sequence or similar construction of other works that are said to *contextualize* it, or most persistently to the, author who is reputed to be the father and owner of the work. "As for the Text, it reads without the inscription of the Father" (161), Barthes declares, alluding here to the argument of his essay "The Death of the Author," which is both his most widely read and his most widely misread text.

Far more rhetorically aggressive and polemical than "From Work to Text," "The Death of the Author" (1968), which had been published three years earlier, announces the passing of the concepts of the author and of literature, and their replacements by the scriptor and by writing.[10] The author, like the concept of man that Foucault saw rising out of the Renaissance and beginning to set in modern times, assumes the possibility of determining the origin and identity of a piece of writing. As "the epitome and culmination of capitalist ideology" (143) for Barthes (here echoing Althusser), the idea of the author reduces writing to property ownership, literature to positivism, human subjectivity to static identity, criticism to mechanical deciphering, meaning to fixed limitation, and reading to impotent passivity. But with the death of the concept of the author, the powerful revolutionary potential in the text and in writing are released. Here Barthes describes the text as "a multi-dimensional space in which a variety of writings, none of them original, blend and clash." The text is "a tissue of quotations drawn from the innumerable centres of culture" (146). The text liberates "anti-theological activity" and refuses to fix meaning in reason, science, or law (147). The unity of the text, therefore, is to be found not in its origin but in its destination, which is the place of the reader (148).

As is usual with Barthes, his restatement of his position is less explosive in its later version, "From Work to Text," than it was in its earlier formulation. In his later reflections on filiation, he is ready to acknowledge the return of the author, not as a ghost but as a guest in the text. As a "paper-author," the writer's life no longer constitutes the determining origin or faintly concealed code of his work but rather is but one among many fictions that contribute to its meaning. Like Derrida's famous assertion that there is nothing outside the text ["*Il n'y a pas de hors-texte*"],[11] Barthes's announcement of the death of the author is entirely credible in context. For the vast majority of readers the lives of authors are only available by reading biographies, which are obviously texts that have no hieratic status. Barthes's critique of filiation, then, is simply a flamboyant, though necessary, reminder that the world, the *œuvre*, and the author's life coexist in language with the text, its commentaries, and its appropriations.

Reading: Because he has put such emphasis on reading in the shift (or "slide") from work to text and from author to reader, the paragraph Barthes devotes to reading may at first seem rather disappointingly laconic. According to the earlier propositions in his essay, whenever a person picks up a text and begins to read it, a complex multiplicity that constitutes the human subject confronts a network of signifiers that is replete with intertextual references, allusions, and quotations that are intricately woven into the fabric of culture. Thus, virtually everything that stands as knowledge in psychoanalysis, linguistics, anthropology, history, cultural and critical theory, and philosophy is germane to an understanding of reading. But Barthes begins instead with the disarming observation that "structurally, there is no difference between 'cultured' reading and casual reading in trains" (162). Like ordinary-language philosophy, Barthes's purpose here is not to disparage informed or "cultural" reading but rather to point out the richness and significance in all reading experience. To this end, he offers three positive observations and concludes with a metaphor for reading. His positive claims are that the implications of the continuity of writing and reading needs to be recognized, especially by educators in democracies; that reading is not playing with a text but rather the active practice of reproducing the polysemous play of the text; that reading as practice requires rereading, in which the text is played much as a performer plays a musical score.

The metaphor of reading as musical performance alludes in some important ways to Barthes's essay "Musica Practica," which sets out to distinguish between the music one listens to and the music one plays. Reading that simply relates the text to personal experience as an "inner *mimesis*" (162) is analogous to passive listening. But music and texts that are played are not simply auditory; rather they employ the whole body: "seated at the keyboard or the music stand, the body controls, conducts, co-ordinates, having itself to transcribe what it reads, making sound and meaning, the body as inscriber and not just transmitter, simple receiver" (149). In order to develop this idea, Barthes proposes a remarkably compelling theory of two Beethovens: On the one hand, there is Beethoven as free, Romantic hero, artistic Titan, and musical demiurge. The bodily strivings of this Romantic Beethoven are total to the point that he makes it impossible for the amateur to play his music with any real satisfaction. Indeed, his music reaches into the inaudible, into a region where "hearing is not the *exact* locality" (152). On the other hand, there is the

Beethoven of the *Diabelli Variations*, whose music can be grasped, according to Barthes, neither by hearing nor by playing but by reading. It is at this point that, by drawing his theory of reading into his account of Beethoven's music, Barthes fully elaborates his musical metaphor:

> This is not to say that one has to sit with a Beethoven score and get from it an inner recital (which would still remain dependent on the old animistic fantasy); it means that with respect to this music one must put oneself in the position or, better, in the activity of an operator, who knows how to displace, assemble, combine, fit together; in a word (if it is not too worn out), who knows how to structure (very different from constructing or reconstructing in the classic sense). Just as the reading of the modern text (such at least as it may be postulated) consists not in receiving, in knowing or in feeling that text, but in writing it anew, in crossing its writing with a fresh inscription, so too reading this Beethoven is *to operate* his music, to draw it (it is willing to be drawn) into an unknown *praxis* (153).

Indeed, a defining characteristic of the text is that it demands "a fresh inscription" as part of the experience of being read. The future of the text is a new text into which its predecessor is absorbed. For Barthes, boredom is the inability to "produce the text" (163) by a combined process of reading, critical appropriation, and writing.

Pleasure: Barthes's brief comments on pleasure in "From Work to Text" lay the foundation for his book *The Pleasure of the Text* (1973), which he was to publish two years later. In his preliminary theory of textual pleasure, Barthes simply distinguishes between works that give pleasure in being consumed – such as the novels of Proust, Flaubert, Balzac, and Dumas – and the texts of *jouissance* that stimulate new writing. The recognition of one's remoteness from works of the first sort is a sign of one's modernity; whereas texts of the second sort (here he gives no examples) constitute "that space where no language has a hold over any other, where languages circulate" (164).

The Pleasure of the Text explores an admittedly ambiguous and precarious distinction between texts of pleasure and texts of bliss.[12] Texts of pleasure, while they satisfy and grant euphoria, come from culture and do not break with it. In Julia Kristeva's terms, they do not constitute a revolutionary poetics.[13] The practice of reading these texts is therefore comfortable. In contrast, texts of bliss impose a state of loss (or desire) on the reader. They discomfort and unsettle the reader's historical, cultural, and psychological assumptions. Furthermore, they disrupt the reader's tastes, memories, values, and relation to language. When readers respond to both kinds of text, as

Barthes repeatedly confesses he does, they participate both in the hedonism and the destruction of culture; they enjoy the consistency of self while simultaneously seeking its loss; they are thus both psychologically and culturally split (PT 14). In his anticipation of the question, What is this view of the text set over against?, Barthes imagines those who would constitute and those who would oppose a "Society of the Friends of the Text." The enemies of such a society would include all of those who would foreclose the text and its pleasure "by cultural conformism," by the promotion of a "mystique" of literature, "by political moralism," "by criticism of the signifier," "by destruction of discourse," and by the "loss of verbal desire" (PT 14–15). The Society of Friends of the Text, on the other hand, would be a collection of small groups celebrating an affinity of passion, difference, and free expression. Here Barthes's principal image of hedonistic textuality is derived from Fourier's phalansterianism, which was a scheme of life devoted to the free expression of passion in the belief that such freedom would promote social harmony. Small affinity groups (or phalanges) were to occupy a phalanstery, a beautiful residence in the center of a self-sustaining tract of land. In such a society the celebration of difference would replace conflict, which Barthes, apparently disagreeing here with Foucault, sees as nothing but a morally rigidified state of difference.[14] For this society, the text is not a dialogue (as Kristeva, by way of Bakhtin, had argued)[15] because in its modes of pleasure the text is asocial but not neuter. The members of the Society do not assume that the text is an active object and the reader a passive subject (PT 16), but because the text has the figure of an "erotic body" with "its own ideas," the critic is a voyeur (PT 17).

Barthes concedes that there is at least one problem in his theory of pleasure that may be specific to the French language, which lacks an umbrella term for pleasure and bliss, contentment and rapture. But this problem may also be emblematic of textuality because pleasure can be expressed in words while bliss cannot. The realm of pleasure can be rendered in language. There writers and readers accept and affirm the letter; and writers have the right and power to express it. There the writer loves language, not speech, and criticism is able to deal with the texts the writer produces. The realm of bliss, on the other hand is populated by such diverse writers as Bataille, Sade, Sollers, Sarduy, Robbe-Grillet, Mallarmé, Nietzsche, Fourier, and Poe. Because bliss cannot be rendered in language, writers and readers contend with the impossible text. Here the text is outside both pleasure and criticism. Here one cannot speak on or about the text, only within it, by a "desperate plagiarism." And here the "void of bliss" is hysterically affirmed (PT 21).

Barthes concludes his essay by denying that he has articulated a theory of the text, not simply because he has pieced together ideas that other writers have developed but also because the text always subverts any meta-language designed to contain it. For that reason any discursive theory of the text would necessarily be subject to the destabilizing critical processes of textuality itself. That means that the only place where a theory of the text can be realized is within writing itself. It would, however, be a complete betrayal of Barthes's thought to read this observation as though it were a claim that literature or other forms of writing are already necessarily theoretical, enabling any piece of writing to know itself. Quite the contrary: There remains a persistent resistance within literature to recognizing the critical theoretical potential in texts, as though the ultimate achievement of literature were to stifle the drive to knowledge and the desire for the real. The continuing search in Barthes's later essays and books was for a way to overcome that resistance, to transcend the imaginary, and to encounter the sign of the real in the fact of human mortality that is always just on the other side of thought.

NOTES

1   Roland Barthes, *Image – Music – Text*, trans. Stephen Heath (London: Fontana, 1977), p. 179. All further references to this book will be by page numbers in parentheses.
2   Michael Moriarty, *Roland Barthes* (Stanford: Stanford University Press, 1991), pp. 10–11. The most important attack on Barthes was launched by Raymond Picard in *Nouvelle critique ou nouvelle imposture* (Paris, 1965), to which Barthes responded with *Critique et vérité* (Paris: Seuil, 1966).
3   Michel-Antoine Burnier and Patrick Rambaud, *Le Roland Barthes sans perne* (Paris: Ballard, 1978). See Jonathan Culler, *Barthes* (London: Fontana, 1983), pp. 9–23, for an excellent account of Barthes's reputation.
4   *Critical Essays*, trans. Richard Howard (Evanston, IL: Northwestern University Press, 1972), p. 260. For a comprehensive bibliography of Barthes's publications, see Sanford Freedman and Carole Anne Taylor, *Roland Barthes: A Bibliographical Reader's Guide* (New York: Garland, 1983).
5   Thomas Kuhn, *The Structure of Scientific Revolutions* (Chicago: University of Chicago Press, 1962).
6   For an excellent account of Barthes's complex but direct response to Saussure, see Moriarty, *Barthes*, pp. 73–90.
7   Cf. Jacques Derrida, "Structure, Sign, and Play in the Discourse of the Human Sciences," in *Writing and Difference*, trans. Alan Bass (Chicago: University of Chicago Press, 1978), esp. pp. 278–9.
8   Ibid.

9   For a discussion of "poststructuralism" as metaphor, see Michael Payne (ed.), *Dictionary of Cultural and Critical Theory* (Oxford: Blackwell, 1996), pp. 436–7.

10 See also F. Ferrara, *The Origin and Decline of the Concept of "Literature"* (Naples: Instituto Universitario Orientale, 1973).

11 Jacques Derrida, *Of Grammatology*, trans. Gayatri Chakravorty Spivak (Baltimore: Johns Hopkins University Press, 1976), p. 158.

12 Roland Barthes, *The Pleasure of the Text*, trans. Richard Miller (New York: Hill and Wang, 1975). References will be in parentheses and abbreviated PT.

13 See *Revolution in Poetic Language*, trans. Margaret Waller (New York: Columbia University Press, 1978), esp. pp. 197–233. Kristeva's recent work on Proust indicates her disagreement with Barthes's judgment that his fiction offers merely pleasure.

14 Conflict is one of the three epistemes discussed by Foucault in *The Order of Things*: see the discussion of this text below.

15 See *Revolution in Poetic Language*, p. 178.

2

Foucault's "Nietzsche, Genealogy, History"

Since his death in 1984, Michel Foucault's reputation and influence have steadily grown to such a point that he is now generally considered one of the most important thinkers of the twentieth century.[1] Three major biographical studies have recently appeared: Didier Eribon's *Michel Foucault* places the details of Foucault's intellectual career in the context of the French academic institutions within which it took shape, including the École Normale Supérieure (ENS), where he studied, and the Collège de France, to which he was appointed after the death of Jean Hyppolite. David Macey's *The Lives of Michel Foucault* constructs a grand narrative of Foucault's life and an impressively detailed chronological account of his more than 400 publications, managing to overcome many of the obstacles that Foucault himself put in the way of his biographers. Appearing almost simultaneously with Macey's book, James Miller's *The Passion of Michel Foucault* fashions a secular and contemporary saint's life for Foucault by looking back on his writings from the perspective of the circumstances of his sadomasochistic experiments with the pleasures of pain, his lifelong meditations on mortality, and his death from AIDS.[2] Despite the importance of these recent books for securing his enduring reputation, 20 years earlier Foucault was already being celebrated by Althusser as a master of thought who taught how to read works of knowledge.[3]

An extraordinarily careful and critically imaginative reader, Foucault carried forward in his own work a legacy that he inherited from his mentors. These included not only Jean Hyppolite, who taught students preparing to enter the ENS to read *The Phenomenology of Spirit* with as much attention to Hegel's language as one might devote to the reading of Mallarmé's poetry, but also Jacques Lacan, who heralded a return to the writings of Freud and who insisted that students of psychoanalysis begin to recover Freud's poetics by actually reading what he wrote; and Louis Althusser, who conducted a collaborative, systematic, and scientific reading of Marx's *Capital* without losing sight of the fact that Marx was first and foremost a writer. But since Hyppolite, Lacan, and Althusser produced major critical texts themselves, Foucault also inherited from them the problem of belatedness, of how to be true to their critical example without his merely imitating them. It was not enough for him to understand critically what he read in their books, which would simply have been to repeat what they had already done. Foucault was also determined to assimilate the power of their knowledge in such a way as to be able to live what he knew. In reaching this determination, he had been struck by a passage in Nietzsche's *Untimely Meditations*, which concludes: "Be yourself! All you are now doing, thinking, desiring, is not you yourself."

On March 4, 1972, a public conversation took place between Foucault and Deleuze, which was recorded and later published under the title "Intellectuals and Power."[5] At that time Foucault was well known as the author of several influential critical studies of asylums, hospitals, and other institutions, as well as of the best-selling book *The Order of Things*. Toward the end of the conversation, Foucault said,

> Isn't [the] difficulty of finding adequate forms of struggle a result of the fact that we continue to ignore the problem of power? After all, we had to wait until the nineteenth century before we began to understand the nature of exploitation, and to this day, we have yet to fully comprehend the nature of power. It may be that Marx and Freud cannot satisfy our desire for understanding this enigmatic thing which we call power, which is at once visible and invisible, present and hidden, ubiquitous. Theories of government and the traditional analyses of their mechanisms certainly don't exhaust the field where power is exercised and where it functions. The question of power remains a total enigma. Who exercises power? And in what sphere? We now know with reasonable certainty who exploits others, who receives the profits, which people are involved, and we know how these funds are reinvested. But as for power . . . (213).

Because power remained such an enigma, even the revolutionary struggles that took place in Paris during May 1968 seemed then to Foucault superficial and inadequate. And if Marx and Freud – for all they had taught about exploitation and repression – could not satisfy his desire to understand power, who could? But as with all public conversations and published interviews, there was something almost transparently theatrical about this one. Foucault and Deleuze were discussing Nietzsche without mentioning his name. During the previous year Foucault had published "Nietzsche, Genealogy, History" in homage to Hyppolite; and Deleuze's book *Nietzsche and Philosophy* had appeared ten years earlier.

It is not that Nietzsche in any sense had solved the problem of power for Foucault and that power was not for that reason really any longer an enigma for him. Rather the question was how to read Nietzsche and how to understand his thinking about the power of knowledge. Foucault's determination to understand the demands that power makes on knowledge – and reciprocally, how knowledge is also a form of power – was already underway when he had written the essay "Nietzsche, Genealogy, History." More than any other short text he wrote, that piece still provides the best introduction to Foucault's thought and the most direct means of access to his investigation of the relationship between power and knowledge.[6]

Before turning in some detail to that essay, however, it may be well to mention two seemingly antithetical, even contradictory, features of Foucault's philosophical style, one concerning his manner of reading and the other his manner of writing. Like Nietzsche, Foucault was an exceptionally patient, slow, and "genealogical" reader. For both of them, reading well, as Nietzsche put it in his 1886 Preface to *The Dawn*, "means reading slowly, deeply, with consideration and caution."[7] To read as Nietzsche advocated requires not just reading with sufficient care to recheck what comes before in the same text, seeing if one understands the earlier portions properly in terms of what comes in the later ones. It also requires a determination to place what one is reading in relation to the previous works of the writer and to see where the writer's work goes on from there. Furthermore, it involves uncovering, approximately as an archaeologist does, what lies buried beneath what is now being read, finding, for example, not just Nietzsche beneath Foucault, but also Nietzsche's reading of the history of philosophy beneath that, and his meticulous classical scholarship working even further down. (Nietzsche's academic appointment at the University of Basel was, after all, to a chair in classical philology, not philosophy.) Perhaps even more difficult is the task of discovering buried quotations or implicit, uncited allusions to previous readers in a given text. By this means, for example, the reader of Foucault suddenly discovers that Foucault, without being explicit about it, is looking at Nietzsche through a lens supplied to him by Heidegger, if for no other reason than to be able to recognize the particular distortion that lens creates. There is nothing hasty or haphazard about this kind of reading. It requires patient sifting and a careful regard for contextual strata, not an abandonment to what may appear to be an aphoristic invitation to free-play with textual shards.[8] If pursued as the texts of Nietzsche and Foucault demand, reading amounts to sustained contact with the gritty texture of thought itself and to feeling its often compelling power.

Foucault, by way of Nietzsche, wants his reader in turn to be in touch with knowledge and to know the disturbing truth of its power. But as so often with Nietzsche, the aphoristic structure of his texts tempts his readers to do precisely what he despises: to read quickly, haphazardly, and indelicately. As though to provide a check on the misperception of his own textual forms, Nietzsche often made his expectations of readers explicit, as he does in these three passages from texts to which Foucault refers in "Nietzsche, Genealogy, History":

[1] When I imagine a perfect reader, he always turns into a monster of courage and curiosity; moreover, supple, cunning, cautious; a born adventurer and discoverer. (N, 264)

[2] Scholars who at bottom do little nowadays but thumb books – philologists, at a moderate estimate, about 200 a day – ultimately lose entirely their capacity to think for themselves. When they don't thumb, they don't think. They *respond* to a stimulus (a thought they have read) whenever they think – in the end, they do nothing but react. Scholars spend all of their energies on saying Yes and No, on criticism of what others have thought – they themselves no longer think. (N, 253)

[3] . . . One thing is necessary above all if one is to practice reading as an *art* . . . something that has been unlearned most thoroughly nowadays – and therefore it will be some time before my writings are "readable" – something for which one has almost to be a cow and in any case *not* a "modern man": *rumination.* (N, 23)

Even though Foucault was an active, eager, and inspiring model of the engaged intellectual, often literally putting his body at risk for those who were mentally and physically ill and for those imprisoned for crimes or for challenging the power of the state, he was, nevertheless, a slow, thoughtful, and methodical reader. Nietzschean rumination was critical for his reading and thinking.

As though in an effort to bring his activism and his thinking as close together as possible, Foucault's texts are electric with rhetorical power. Sometimes this is the power of newly discovered buried information that his painstaking researches have unearthed concerning the history of asylums, prisons, and medical practices. But more often it is the power of Foucault's life of "passion," a word that James Miller, somewhat sensationally but nevertheless accurately, has elevated to a christological sense of ecstatic self-sacrifice that is more than desire or a manifestation of the Freudian instinct of epistemophilia. Indeed, it is a kind of intellectual transfiguration or *jouissance.* Here, for example, is a brief passage from Foucault's commentary on Flaubert's *The Temptation of Saint Anthony*, which is in the mode of such passion:

The "temptation" of Saint Anthony is the double fascination exercised upon Christianity by the sumptuous spectacle of its past and the limitless acquisitions of its future . . . *The Temptation* does not mask reality in its glittering images, but reveals the image of an image in the realm of truth. Even in its state of primitive purity, Christianity was formed by the dying reflections of an older world, formed by the feeble light it projected upon the still grey shadows of a nascent world. (F, 103)

Here, as is typical of Foucault, his carefully ruminative reading ignites his passion. His intellectual power, however, is not just derived from that of the texts he reads; it is not just Flaubert's or Nietzsche's power recycled. Instead, his is the power of a critical reader's knowledge that comes from what he takes to be "an image in the realm of truth." Although Foucault was a meticulous textual archaeologist, he had no more patience than Nietzsche with merely repetitive philology. But he was no less contemptuous of naive activism that is born of the thoughtless conviction that what is good can be immediately and unproblematically known and that evil can be vanquished with no more than good intentions and simple determination.

Much of Foucault's "Nietzsche, Genealogy, History" was based on the lectures he had attempted to give after the University of Paris was split up into a number of campuses around the city, following the events of May 1968. Although he headed the department of philosophy at Vincennes – which has been described as a "ghetto of almost total internal freedom," where, for example, Lacan's daughter, in an unreflective enactment of Althusser's politics, said she tried to make the university function "worse and worse" in an effort to bring down one portion of the apparatus of the state[9] – Foucault nevertheless made a determined effort to continue his scholarly teaching. "In a place where one was theoretically free to say anything," as Alan Sheridan has observed, "but where in practice everyone said much the same thing, if only because conformism was indispensable to being heard at all, it was a brave spirit who dared to speak well of Nietzsche, let alone devote an entire course to his philosophy."[10]

At first glance the essay "Nietzsche, Geneaology, History" appears to be about only three words that Nietzsche uses in accounting for the history of morality. These words are *Ursprung* or origin, *Herkunft* or descent, and *Entstehung* or emergence. It is as though in his essay Foucault is confronting Nietzsche, the philologist who was contemptuous of philologists, with a prime instance of Nietzsche's own philological work. Or perhaps it is that by reading Nietzsche's *The Genealogy of Morals* in the context of *The Gay Science*; *Human, All Too Human*; *The Dawn*; *Beyond Good and Evil*; and *Untimely Meditations*, Foucault is carrying forward or making explicit what was left incomplete or implicit in Nietzsche's texts. Initially this is a question of how to read

Nietzsche as Nietzsche seemed to want to be read, however doubtful he was that he would ever have such a reader as Foucault. In a passage in the section of *Ecce Homo* entitled "Why I Write Such Good Books," for example, Nietzsche begins by contemptuously claiming that no one can get more out of books than what he already knows, only to write in the next sentence about an extreme and thus privileged case in which "a book speaks of nothing but events that lie altogether beyond the possibility of any frequent or even rare experience – that it is the first language for a new series of experiences" (N, 261). In what follows this passage, Nietzsche in effect demands that his books be read in the impossible, infrequent, or rare way of providing language for a series of experiences that his reader has not yet had. Although Foucault does not cite this passage from *Ecce Homo*, this is the way he actually reads Nietzsche. But he sets out to read Nietzsche in all his strangeness in order to discover in Nietzsche's writing about history a new way to understand history. Foucault, therefore, takes his own reader into the thick forest of textuality to find there the path that will lead to the truth of history. As he undertakes this journey in "Nietzsche, Genealogy, History," Foucault offers as signposts the seven numbered sections of his essay, to which we now turn.

1. Foucault begins by warning his reader that "genealogy is gray, meticulous, and patiently documentary" (F, 139), which already marks his essay as an understated manifesto for genealogy, in contrast to the much more flamboyant manifesto for grammatology (or deconstruction) that Derrida had published four years earlier.[11] The documents with which genealogy works are "entangled," "confused," and multilayered, having been "scratched over and recopied many times." They thus require laborious deciphering, as though each one constitutes a site for an archaeological dig. Not far from Foucault's attention here is the familiar archaeological image in Freud's *Civilization and Its Discontents*, by which Freud struggles to avoid any progressivist metaphor for the structure of the mind, opting instead for the image of Rome as a multilayered site, where the inscribed remains of the past can be uncovered beneath the surface of the present.[12] Accordingly, Foucault reaffirms Nietzsche's rejection in *The Genealogy of Morals* of the mistaken notion that the history of morality develops linearly in the direction of an end or that its function is utilitarian by promoting a specified outcome. Such errors are based on a failure to attend to the circuitous ways of language and desire, which genealogy is determined to follow without any expectation of finality. In carrying out its investigations of the indirections of language and desire, genealogy turns to what history has despised or neglected, much as deconstruction finds itself at home in the margins of philosophy. Not only does genealogy prize sentiments and instincts which have been neglected by

history, but also significant absences and silences in the records of the past. In these excavatory efforts, however, genealogy does not work in opposition to history as such, only to history's determined search for origins. Although Foucault leaves this implicit in his argument, genealogy deeply shares deconstruction's suspicion of the metaphysical fiction that language can make present what it signifies, that desire seeks to end itself in satisfaction, and that origins can be recovered.[13] Traditional history – the work of Paul Rée is Nietzsche's example – has often promised to make the past present in current historiography and to trace the trajectory of the past from origins to emergence. It is no accident, therefore, that the word "history" has come to refer both to events and to what historians write about events.

2.   Having introduced the project of genealogy as a polemic against traditional historiography – in keeping with the genre of *The Genealogy of Morals*, which Nietzsche subtitles *A Polemic* (*Eine Streitschrift*) – Foucault proceeds to a critical assessment of Nietzsche's language. Nietzsche's word for origin (*Ursprung*) is employed in two ways. Sometimes it is "unstressed" and appears interchangeably with various synonyms for "beginning." At key points in his argument, however, Nietzsche stresses the word, often by using it ironically. In his preface to the *Genealogy*, for example, he recalls, as a boy of 13, attributing the origin of evil to God in a delightful outburst of adolescent blasphemy (N, 17). But when he refers to his current efforts to examine the descent of moral preconceptions, the word he uses is *Herkunft*. Since Paul Rée, Nietzsche's model of the traditional historian, had read Darwin (N, 21), Nietzsche's move from *origin* to *descent* has considerable Darwinian resonance. The genealogist, who investigates descent rather than origin, would seem always to be a polemicist who pricks inflated and high-minded explanations. When he looks behind reason and liberty, for example, what he finds is that reason, truth, and scientific precision spring from scholarly passion and that the concept of liberty is an "invention of the ruling classes" (F, 142).

Why challenge the pursuit of origins? First, because of its metaphysical pretensions. To pursue origins requires the belief that it is possible to "capture the exact essence of things, their purest possibilities, and their carefully protected identities." The genealogist, refusing to leap out of history into a timeless essentialism, discovers in historical beginnings not an "inviolable identity" but a disparity of particulars, each with its own set of receding disparities. Second, Nietzsche and Foucault challenge the pursuit of origins because of its endless repetition of an unexamined myth: "The origin always precedes the Fall. It comes before the body, before the world and time; it is associated with the gods, and its story is always sung as a theogony" (F, 143).

The genealogist, however, sees this myth as a lofty fabrication and knows that historical beginnings are corporeal, lowly, derisive, and ironic, recalling the Darwinian monkey that pulls at Zarathustra's coattails. In this sense a historical beginning does not constitute a temporally transcendent, fixed point of origin but rather a focal point for the genealogist's investigation and the first episode in his subsequent narrative.[14] Finally, Nietzsche and Foucault challenge the pursuit of origins because it places truth beyond or outside of history. Since "the origin lies at a place of inevitable loss, the point where the truth of things corresponded to a truthful discourse" (F, 143), then nothing that can be said about it can be true, historical constructions always being necessarily retrospects, backward glances from displaced points in time. In a futile effort to extricate himself from the dilemma he has created, the traditional historian invents a theory of language that is overburdened by an impossible metaphysics, claiming that language itself makes the past present. Another myth is thus required in a desperate effort to salvage the truth of history. This is the myth of the history of truth, which holds that truth was first revealed to men of wisdom, then carried off and made unattainable for others by men of piety, and finally disgarded altogether as useless, superfluous, and contradictory. By not abandoning the vicissitudes of history for the chimera of origin, the genealogist cultivates "the details and accidents that accompany every beginning," is "scrupulously attentive to their petty malice," and "awaits their emergence, once unmasked, as the face of the other" (F, 144). In this sense the genealogist of morals maintains the particularity of difference and a necessary distance between himself and the object of his investigation, refusing to become so completely identified with it that its otherness disappears in some grand narcissistic act of incorporation. Although the genealogist eschews the loftiness of myth for the subversiveness of irony, his appropriate aesthetic mode would seem nevertheless to be the sublime, both because the sublime refuses to collapse the object or field of perception into the subject and because in maintaining that difference the genealogist espouses a compact between ethics and aesthetics.[15] Ethics, like the sublime, requires the distinctiveness of the other. For this reason the physical body in its varying conditions of health and disease, weakness and strength, vulnerability and resistance is fundamental to the work of the genealogist. Rather than being a stable human reality, however, the body has been variously designated and delineated by the discourses of biology and medicine.

In his assertion of the genealogical importance of the body, Foucault is already forecasting his later turn to the history of sexuality, which occupied the last years of his life. The three domains of Foucault's analytical work have been usefully designated as modalities of power, systems of knowledge, and the self's relationship to itself.[16] It is a mistake, however, to think of these domains as discrete, sequential concerns, as though suddenly in the final phase of his life Foucault had discovered his body in the gay bars and bath-houses of San Francisco. Such is Edward Said's recent ungenerous dismissal of Foucault, whose work had been the foundation for Said's theories of beginnings and Orientalism.

> Foucault . . . turned his attention away from the oppositional forces in modern society which he had studied for their undeterred resistance to exclusion and confinement – delinquents, poets, outcasts, and the like – and decided that since power was everywhere it was probably better to concentrate on the local micro-physics of power that surround the individual. The self was therefore to be studied, cultivated, and, if necessary, refashioned and constituted.[17]

As though anticipating the possibility of such a misreading, in the final volume of his *History of Sexuality*, apropos of his discussion of the importance of medicine to the ancient Romans, Foucault insists that

> medicine was not conceived simply as a technique of intervention, relying, in cases of illness, on remedies and operations. It was also supposed to define, in the form of a corpus of knowledge and rules, a way of living, a reflective mode of relation to oneself, to one's body, to food, to wakefulness and sleep, to the various activities, and to the environment. Medicine was expected to propose, in the form of regimen, a voluntary and rational structure of conduct.[18]

It is important to observe that Foucault is here writing about the ethical underpinnings of Roman medicine, rather than simply recording their exotic mores. When Foucault decided to call one of his last interviews "Genealogy of Ethics," he was chosing the equivalent of Kant's word for ethics (*Sitte*) instead of Nietzsche's more anthropologically encompassing word for morals (*Moral*).[19] Although Foucault is investigating the ethical practices of the ancient world in his *History of Sexuality*, he nonetheless works to preserve Kant's turn from the ancient ethical focus on the good life to the internaliza-tion of ethics and its dependence both on reason and the sublime. Again anticipating this later argument, Foucault concludes the second section of his affirmation of genealogy in "Nietzsche, Genealogy, History" with a series of medical images: the genealogist is allied with the doctor; he must be able to "diagnose the illnesses of the body," unlike the metaphysician who claims to deal only with the soul; and history itself is that concrete body, complete with its own signs of disease and health (F, 144–5).

3. Foucault opens the third section of his essay by announcing that Nietzsche's words for descent (*Herkunft*) and emergence (*Entstehung*) better suggest the project of genealogy than his word for origin (*Ursprung*). Descent assumes the offspring of the loins, of bloodlines, and of a bodily tradition. It is at this point in his argument that Foucault's careful attention to the poetics of Nietzschean word choice becomes reminiscent of Heideggerian etymological construction, and it is almost as though Foucault were reading back through Heidegger's massive study of Nietzsche in order to get to Nietzsche's own text.[20] Such a reading strategy produces a purposeful disparity, which is precisely what the pursuit of origins abhorred. Foucault wants to suggest that descent assumes not a single bloodline, much less a monolithic sense of what is Greek or English or German. Thus, in an extraordinarily bold argumentative stroke Nietzsche traces the racial diversity and complexity of the Germans (N, 30–1), which leads Foucault to observe that the theory that Germans possessed a "double soul" is itself a futile attempt to "master the racial disorder from which they had formed themselves" (F, 145). From this overthrow of identity and celebration of disparity descends the image of the dissociated self, or what Lacan prefers to call the subject.[21]

Given its focus on descent, genealogy deals with the multiplicity of an "exteriority of accidents" that produced what continues to exist in the present. It does not, however, suppose a unity of the past with the present or presume to map a people's destiny. Rather, the structure of descent is a highly "unstable assemblage of faults, fissures, and heterogeneous layers that threaten the fragile inheritor from within or from underneath" (F, 146). Genealogy makes no attempt to stabilize this structure, to shore it up or to erect new foundations beneath it. Instead, in the course of its investigations it further "disturbs what was previously considered immobile," "fragments what was thought unified," and "shows the heterogeneity of what was imagined consistent with itself" (F, 147). Once again, Foucauldian genealogical history closely parallels Derridean deconstructive grammatology. But what the genealogist reads is the text of events "inscribed" on the body, thus situating his analysis within the "articulation" of the body and its history. His task then "is to expose a body totally imprinted by history and the process of history's destruction of the body" (F, 148).

Foucault does not elaborate further here on the textual history of the body. Such a task of illustration was, however, to be carried out in encyclopaedic detail in the three volumes of his *History of Sexuality*. One of the hundreds of examples offered there is Galen's account of the physiological processes of human sexual activity. Like other ancient authorities, Galen was convinced that, despite the genital localization of erotic pleasure, sexual activity engaged the entire body. Disagreeing with Aristotle's notion that sperm is produced as part of the final stage of digestion, he argued in the manner of an early genealogist that sperm has more than one source. In part, he thought, sperm is a product of a "coction" in the blood that flows through the spermatic channels. But the sperm also requires the presence of *pneuma*, which is produced in the labyrinthine passages of the brain. *Pneuma* is the spirit or essence of the person that must in part be conveyed to the offspring without draining the parent. During the sexual act the testicles draw the dew-like droplets of sperm from the blood, beginning with the genital veins and eventually rising up to withdraw it from the entire body. If, however, such expenditure is prolonged and the whole body is completely drained of its seminal fluids, then the body becomes sapped of its spiritual vitality. The all-encompassing bodily pleasure of sexuality can thus end in death. Conversely, when *pneuma* is congested in the brain, the result is an epileptic convulsion rather than orgasm.[22] Foucault's reading of such texts as Galen's produces a historical reconfiguration of the body, which has massive consequences for rethinking the cultural discourses of the past.

4.   Having affirmed Nietzsche's association of genealogy with the delineation of descent rather than with the search for pre-temporal origin, Foucault forestalls a possible misreading of descent by recalling Nietzsche's suspicion about emergence. Just as traditional historiography has attempted to escape from the flow of history into origin, so also has it endeavored to stop that flow by believing in final outcomes or "moments of arising" (*Entstehung*) in historical processes. Although particular historical developments may appear as culminations, Foucault reads Nietzsche as insisting that they are merely the "current episodes in a series of subjugations." Descent is neither an "uninterrupted continuity" nor a process leading to a definitive emergence (F, 148). The idea of emergence is important, however, in that it exposes the dynamics of contending forces that activate history. Activity, for Nietzsche, is a fundamental concept of life (N, 78). One force may contend with another, divide and contend with itself, fall into lassitude, or regain strength. Emergence, however, is simply the moment of the eruption of force, which necessarily and impersonally occurs in what Nietzsche calls an interstice or non-place. The drama of subjugation is endlessly replayed there, not in order to reach a point at which combat gives way to reciprocity or war submits to law. The total warfare of contending forces does not simply exhaust itself in a contradiction that positively gives rise to peace and law; rather, the law itself continues the endless play of domination. Law is the systematic instillation of violence, not its end. Understanding the rules by which violence operates is therefore crucial. Not only do the successes of history go to those who can

manipulate the system of rules, but also interpretation, itself a play of domination, is the violent appropriation of such rules, which lack any essential meaning (F, 151).

As itself a mode of dominating interpretation, genealogy merges with the forces it sets out to anatomize. This, at last, points to a purposeful ambiguity in the word "history," where the record merges with the event and consequently becomes an event itself. Although Foucault does not cite this particular passage, Nietzsche in the second of the *Untimely Meditations* argues that history (first as record, then as event) can actually operate in the manner of a parasite or vampire that drains vitality from its object of study (his examples are then recent histories of Christianity and of German music).[23] What infuriates Nietzsche about this is that history for him is a living organism, but as such it is constantly vulnerable to the deadly dissecting assaults of the professional historian. Indeed, history has made life sick, Nietzsche argues, in the visionary conclusion of his essay "On the uses and disadvantages of history for life":

> It is sick, this unchained life, and needs to be cured. It is sick with many illnesses and not only with the memory of its chains – what chiefly concerns us here is that it is suffering from the *malady of history*. Excess of history has attacked life's plastic powers, it no longer knows how to employ the past as a nourishing food.[24]

The crucial functions of the genealogist, then, are to diagnose the illnesses of history (F, 145) and to teach the ways of recovering the nutritiousness of the past.

5.   Foucault has so far carried out a systematic examination of Nietzsche's historiographical terminology according to principles that Foucault called "archaeological," a term he tactfully avoids here, doubtless in order to keep Nietzsche's language under investigation without mixing in extraneous bits of his own. The archaeology of knowledge is for Foucault a distinctive departure from the history of ideas, which he describes this way:

> [The archaeology of knowledge] recounts the by-ways and margins of history. Not the history of the sciences, but that of imperfect, ill-based knowledge, which could never in the whole of its long, persistent life attain the form of scientificity (the history of alchemy rather than chemistry, or animal spirits or phrenology rather than physiology, the history of atomistic themes rather than physics). The history of those shady philosophies that haunt literature, art, the sciences, law, ethics, and even man's daily life; the history of those age-old themes that are never crystallized in a rigorous and individual system,

but which have formed the spontaneous philosophy of those who did not philosophize.[25]

Foucault finds Nietzsche carrying out such an archaeology of knowledge in his critiques of history. The thing that is so compelling about their common project, however, is not that they are locating some long forgotten, quaint mode of knowledge out of antiquarian interest. Instead, the conceptual terminology and the structures of thought they interrogate are still embedded in the spontaneous philosophy of much current thought.

Having completed his archaeological excavation of "origin," "descent," and "emergence," Foucault turns to the question of the relationship of genealogy to traditional history. The form of historiography that Nietzsche considered poisonous and deadly was any perspective on the past that attempted to elevate itself above history by reducing temporal diversity to a closed and static entity, by attempting to reconcile the displacements of the past, or by looking for definitive outcomes in episodes of the moment. Such "suprahistorical" perspectives inevitably rest on unexamined assumptions, such as universal truth or transcendent identity. Genealogy refuses such absolutes; but, again like deconstructive grammatology, genealogy turns its own suspecting, liberating, and dissociating glance back upon itself. The effect of this relentlessly self-reflexive critique is that it productively decomposes itself, shatters "the unity of man's being," and in so doing dispels the illusion that the historian of the present can be the sovereign of the past. In a distinct echo of the famous last sentences of *The Order of Things*,[26] Foucault celebrates genealogy's refusal of any constants: "Nothing in man – not even his body – is sufficiently stable to serve as the basis for self-recognition or for understanding other men" (F, 153). Contingency is one of genealogy's few constants.

In its polemical assault on traditional historiography, genealogy produces a new kind of knowledge, which Foucault calls "effective" history. Rather than promoting continuity and understanding, effective history not only celebrates discontinuity but actually produces it. Such knowledge, Foucault abruptly announces, is "made for cutting," which appears to mean that effective history always maintains a sense of difference by dealing with singular events and their unique characteristics.[27] This implies a resistance to the humanistic temptations of traditional history, which presuppose an eternal human essence that lies beneath every cultural and temporal difference. Ruled by chance and the will to power, the world of effective history is a "profusion of entangled events" that do not manifest intention or immutable necessity. Given its emphasis on otherness and discreteness, effective history works within a shortened time span rather than invisioning "lofty epochs" (F, 155). Although it affirms "knowledge as perspective," the perspective effective history takes is openly slanted, judgmental, and value-laden. But by prominently marking its position, it incorporates a genealogy of itself into the knowledge it produces.

6.   Foucault is now in a position to turn his argument in upon itself and to declare that, along with Nietzsche, he has been conducting all along his own genealogical investigation by writing an effective history of historiography. Although traditional history has attempted to be a totalizing discourse, what has always escaped it is itself, especially its errors, reductiveness, and insensitivities. Thus, the historian has been able to mask his demagogy (F, 158). It is revealing in this respect that the emergence of history occurred in nineteenth-century Europe at a time of the bastardized barbarian – as Foucault calls him – who desired to escape into the past. The plebeian historian, from his perspective of distance, at that time turned back longingly to the high civilizations which no longer existed. Historical curiosity thus arose out of decadence, a lack of self-knowledge, and the desire of Europeans to conceal their mixed descent. What Nietzsche clearly saw as he wrote his manifesto for genealogy was the need for history, especially given its circumstances of emergence, to come to know itself.

7.   Foucault concludes with a sketch of the three uses of history and its three Platonic modalities, which may be presented as follows:

	Parodic	*Dissociative*	*Sacrificial*
Directed against	Reality	Identity	Truth
Opposes	History as reminiscence or recognition	History as continuity or tradition	History as knowledge
Nietzschean double	Monumental history	Antiquarian history	Critical history

In the parodic mode, history offers the modern European a number of masks or alternate identities, which serve to hide his own confusion and anonymity. The "new historian" or genealogist knows how to deal with this masquerade. While enjoying it, he pushes it to its limits and prepares "the great carnival of time where masks are constantly reappearing" (F, 161). Wearing this succession of masks further destabilizes an already weak identity; and as the genealogist revels in this carnival, he exposes (unmasks?) monumental history, showing it to be a parody of itself. In history's dissociative mode, the identity beneath the masks is also recognized as a plurality in which "numerous systems interact and compete" (F, 161). In this context the motive of antiquarian history can easily be understood. Its efforts to recover the rooted stability of the soil, the native land, and the native language are desperate efforts to return to stabilizing origins. The genealogist, however, who always works to reveal the heterogeneity of systems, knows that the antiquarian's longing for lost origins simply blocks any sense of identity, however unstable.

In its sacrificial mode, history is at first serenely committed to truth. As it reflects on the forms of what it knows, however, the sacrificial mode discovers that passion, power, and the will to knowledge animate historical consciousness. It then proceeds to strip that consciousness of its pretensions by demonstrating that "all knowledge rests upon injustice"; that "the instinct for knowledge is malicious"; that "knowledge does not achieve a universal truth"; that "it ceaselessly multiplies . . . risk," creating dangers everywhere; that "it releases those elements of itself that are devoted to its subversion and destruction"; and that "it creates a progressive enslavement of the subject to its instinctive violence" (F, 163). Neither Nietzsche nor Foucault avoids the distinct possibility that the sacrificial passion sustaining the desire for knowledge may bring about the extinction of mankind: "to knowledge, no sacrifice is too great" (F, 164). Although *The Genealogy of Morals*, published in 1887, looks back on Nietzsche's meditations on the modalities of history, which he completed in 1874, it is the later text which confronts the possible destruction of the subject who is driven by the will to knowledge.

Foucault does not supply his essay with any neat, prophetic conclusion. To do so would have betrayed his and Nietzsche's rejection of the illusion of a definitive historical emergence. Foucault, however, does not flinch from highlighting the irresistible and possibly destructive power of knowledge. It would, I think, be a mistake to read either Nietzsche or Foucault as equating the will to knowledge with the death instinct. Even Freud left a separate theoretical space for "the instinct for knowledge"[28] although he never gave it the sustained, explicit attention that went to his elucidation of eros and thanatos. Based upon his reading of Nietzsche, however, Foucault devoted most of his work to an investigation of the power of knowledge.

At the time of his death Foucault was at work on his multi-volume history of sexuality, the first installment of which had been published in 1976 as *La Volonté de savoir (The Will to Knowledge)*. Unfortunately, the English title (*The History of Sexuality: An Introduction*) loses the echo of Nietzsche's *The Will to*

Power. Although all of Foucault's genealogical work – from his earlier investigations of the discourses of madness, order, and punishment to his incomplete
history of sexuality – manifest the historiographical suspicions of the essay
"Nietzsche, Genealogy, History," those doubts become lucidly refined in *La
Volonté de savoir*. Virtually everywhere in modern discourses on sexuality,
Foucault recalls, the same story is repeated or taken for granted, a story that
goes like this: Up to the beginning of the seventeenth century a certain
frankness about sexuality was usual in Europe. But with the development of
capitalism in the seventeenth century, repression became an integral part of
the new bourgeois social order. Sexual repression continued to increase until it
reached its greatest point of intensity during the Victorian age. Now, in light
of critical assessments of nineteenth-century culture, new sexual freedom has
become possible once again, resulting in the liberation of the truth of sexuality. But is this story true, Foucault asks, or is its telling yet the latest form of
sexual repression? Modernist discourse, which appears freely to proclaim the
truth of sexuality, is subject to strange and unexpected impasses. Why is it so
pleasurable to proclaim that repression constitutes the relationship between
sex and power? If, in fact, sex is "condemned to prohibition, nonexistence, and
silence, then the mere fact that one is speaking about it has the appearance of
a deliberate transgression."[29] Such is the persistent irony of the sermon that its
effort to proclaim the truth of sin becomes in fact a means of producing its
effects. In order to investigate the circuitous paths of sexuality, Foucault finds
it necessary to define "the regime of power–knowledge–pleasure" that sustains
its discourse.

Because of his life-long concern for the disrupting dynamics of history, it
would doubtless be a betrayal of Foucault's project to read the essay
"Nietzsche, Genealogy, History" as a transcendent, essentialist statement of
the origin of his thought in Nietzsche or to see *The History of Sexuality* as a
definitive emergence, as though it repudiated somehow his earlier archaeological investigations into the discourses of knowledge and substituted for them
some new mode of genealogical critique. That there are only either out-of-
which thinkers or in-to-which thinkers – those bound by the past or wedded
to the future – is a formula that Foucault no less than Nietzsche refused to
credit. In hindsight, however, it does appear that Foucault came to distinguish
archaeology from genealogy, not as a matter of rejecting archaeology but
rather as a matter of affirming the critical intensification of genealogy. As
metaphorical modes for the critique of discourse, the archaeology of the human
sciences excavates and describes what it finds, while geneaology interrogates
the links between those discoveries and systems of power. Alexander Nehamas
has thus observed that:

Genealogy is not, as it sometimes seems to be, a new method of doing history with its own rules and principles; it is rather an effort to take history itself very seriously and to find it where it has least been expected to be. Genealogy takes as its objects precisely those institutions and practices which, like morality, are usually thought to be totally exempt from change and development. It tries to show the way in which they too undergo changes as a result of historical developments. And it also tries to show how such changes escape our notice and how it is often in the interest of these practices to mask their specific historical origins and character. As a result of this, genealogy has direct practical consequences because, by demonstrating the contingent character of the institutions that traditional history exhibits as unchanging, it creates the possibility of altering them.[30]

Nahamas credits Foucault with having an "exact" understanding of Nietzsche's project, when he wrote that the genealogist "finds that there is 'something altogether different' behind things: not a timeless and essential secret, but the secret that they have no essence or that their essence was fabricated in a piecemeal fashion from alien forms" (F, 142). Although the occasion for his writing "Nietzsche, Genealogy, History" was his tribute to his deceased teacher Jean Hyppolite, it also provided Foucault with an opportunity to reflect back on the celebrated work he had completed and to look forward to work that remains, as it will always be, unfinished.

NOTES

1   On the reception of Foucault's thought in North America, see Paul Bové's foreword to Gilles Deleuze, *Foucault*, trans. Seán Hand (Minneapolis: University of Minnesota Press, 1988). A more comprehensive assessment is available in David Couzens Hoy (ed.), *Foucault: A Critical Reader* (Oxford: Blackwell, 1986).
2   Didier Eribon, *Michel Foucault*, trans. Betsy Wing (Cambridge, MA: Harvard University Press, 1991); David Macey, *The Lives of Michel Foucault* (London: Hutchinson, 1993); James Miller, *The Passion of Michel Foucault* (London: Harper Collins, 1993).
3   Louis Althusser and Etienne Balibar, *Reading Capital*, trans. Ben Brewster (London: Verso, 1970), p. 16.
4   Friedrich Nietzsche, *Untimely Meditations*, trans. R.J. Hollingdale (Cambridge: Cambridge University Press, 1983), p. 127. The passage quoted is from the first paragraph of the essay entitled "Schopenhauer as Educator," §1. James Miller (pp. 69, 405n) gives a full account of the importance of this text for Foucault.
5   The French text appeared in *Hommage à Jean Hyppolite* (Paris: Presses Universitaires de France, 1971), pp. 145–72, and the English translation in

Michel Foucault, *Language, Counter-memory, Practice: Selected Essays and Interviews*, ed. Donald F. Bouchard (Ithaca, NY: Cornell University Press, 1977), pp. 204–17. All quotations from Foucault are from this volume, abbreviated to F and further cited by page numbers in parentheses.

6 Hubert L. Dreyfus and Paul Rabinow, apparently with Foucault's endorsement, claim that that this essay was Foucault's first decisive move toward a "satisfactory and self-consciously complex analysis of power" (*Michel Foucault: Beyond Structuralism and Hermeneutics* [Hemel Hempstead: Harvester Wheatsheaf, 1982], p. 106).

7 Quoted by Walter Kaufmann in *On the Genealogy of Morals and Ecce Homo*, trans. Walter Kaufmann and R.J. Hollingdale (New York: Vintage, 1967), p. 22n. All quotations from Nietzsche are from this volume, abbreviated to N and further cited by page numbers in parentheses.

8 Kaufmann's point concerning the importance of reading Nietzsche in context – in opposition to Danto – seems right, though arrogantly stated (N, 22n).

9 Alan Sheridan, *Michel Foucault: The Will to Truth* (London: Routledge, 1980), p. 114. David Macey gives a detailed account of Foucault's work at Vincennes (*The Lives of Michel Foucault*, pp. 208–36.) Judith Miller's remarks were quoted in an article on Vincennes that appeared in *Le Nouvel Observateur*, February 9, 1970.

10 Sheridan, *Faucault*, p. 114.

11 See my *Reading Theory: An Introduction to Lacan, Derrida, and Kristeva* (Oxford: Blackwell, 1993), pp. 110–55.

12 SE, XXI: 69–71. Despite his occasional outbreaks of ambivalence or hostility toward psychoanalysis, Foucault elsewhere credits Freud, along with Marx, as having "established the endless possibility of discourse" (F, 131).

13 Cf. especially Jacques Derrida, *Of Grammatology*, trans. Gayatri Chakravorty Spirak (Baltimore: Johns Hopkins University Press, 1976), pt. I, ch. 1.

14 For a detailed elaboration of this point, see Edward Said, *Beginnings: Intention and Method* (New York: Columbia University Press, 1975). Like Said's book, Hayden White's comprehensive investigations of the narrative forms of historiography work out the implications of Foucault's argument. White has also written one of the best brief introductions to Foucault available ("Michel Foucault," in John Sturrock (ed.), *Structuralism and Since: From Lévi-Strauss to Derrida* [Oxford: Oxford University Press, 1979]).

15 See Slavoj Žižek, *The Sublime Object of Ideology* (London: Verso, 1989), esp. pp. 202–7, and Ian Hacking, "Self-Improvement," in *Foucault: A Critical Reader*, ed. David Couzens Hoy (Oxford: Blackwell, 1986), pp. 238–9.

16 By Arnold Davidson, "Archaeology, Genealogy, Ethics," in *Foucault: A Critical Reader*, p. 221.

17 Edward Said, *Culture and Imperialism* (London: Chatto and Windus, 1993), p. 29. This judgment may be based on a hasty, uncritical acceptance of James Miller's biography (p. 411n).

18 Michael Foucault, *The Care of the Self: The History of Sexuality*, vol. 3, trans. Robert Hurley (London: Penguin, 1990), pp. 99–100.

19   This point is eloquently made by Ian Hacking in "Self-Improvement," pp. 238–9.
20   On Derrida's adoption of a similar strategy, see *Reading Theory*, p. 126.
21   See *Reading Theory*, pp. 26–34 and 91–7.
22   *The Care of the Self*, pp. 108–10. For a brilliant elaboration of Foucault's method, see Peter Brown, *The Body and Society: Men, Women and Sexual Renunciation in Early Christianity* (London: Faber and Faber, 1989).
23   *Untimely Meditations*, pp. 96–7.
24   *Untimely Meditations*, p. 120. Sometimes, as Nietzsche goes on to show, the cure for the malady of history can be as poisonous as the disease.
25   *The Archaeology of Knowledge*, trans. A[lan] S[heridan] (New York: Pantheon, 1972), pp. 136–7.
26   "As the archaeology of our thought easily shows, man is an invention of recent date. And one perhaps nearing its end" (*The Order of Things*, trans. Alan Sheridan [New York: Pantheon, 1970], p. 387).
27   For more on knowledge as cutting, see Foucault's "A Preface to Transgression" (F, 36).
28   For example in SE, VII: 197. For a fuller discussion of epistemophilia, see *Reading Theory*, pp. 83–4, 87–91.
29   *The History of Sexuality: An Introduction*, trans. Robert Hurley (London: Penguin, 1981), p. 6.
30   *Nietzsche: Life as Literature* (Cambridge, MA: Harvard University Press, 1985), p. 112.

3

Althusser's "Ideology and Ideological State Apparatuses"

There are two major obstacles to reading Althusser. The first and more impressive is that his writings have been extraordinarily important for many of the most formidable critical theorists of our time, who have written at length about Althusser either in respectful critical engagement (such as Paul Ricoeur in *Lectures on Ideology and Utopia* and Fredric Jameson in *The Political Unconscious*) or in angry denunciation (such as E. P. Thompson in *The Poverty of Theory*, who calls Althusser's work "unhistorical shit").[1] Althusser's influence was also sufficiently powerful in the thought of an entire generation of French intellectuals – including Derrida, Kristeva, Barthes, Foucault, and Deleuze – that they often employ or respond to his ideas without formal citation or overt acknowledgement. The second obstacle relates either directly or indirectly to the fact that in November 1980, Althusser, apparently in a state of madness, murdered his wife Hélène, who had been his companion for 35 years. At the time of his death in 1992, Althusser's autobiographical writings, which included an agonizingly candid account of his guilt and manic depression, remained unpublished. Although Althusser left no will, his nephew and executor authorized publication of *The Future Lasts Forever: A Memoir* later the same year, under the careful editorship of Olivier Corpet and Yann Moulier Boutang.[2] The temptation to associate Marxism, madness, and murder, while seizing the opportunity to denounce French theoretical work at the same time, was not to be resisted by the popular media around the world. Even the *London Review of Books* devoted a front page to a photograph of Althusser with the caption "The Paris Strangler." A recent book by Geraldine Finn goes even further and angrily claims to have discovered why Althusser killed his wife. Finn's three-part answer is that Althusser's "intellectual practice cannot be separated from his personal and emotion practice"; that there is a direct link that extends from patriarchy and violence to science and knowledge; and that like most French intellectuals (including Barthes, Lacan, Derrida, and Foucault) Althusser supposedly thought politics impossible because "social meanings are both arbitrary and self-referring, social realities

mere simulacra, and [all of us] . . . prisoners of language."[3] Finn's denunciation of Althusser's thought and of what she calls the lyrical nihilism of
"postmodern" French theory is so contemptuous of knowledge that she invents
quotations, ignores biographical information that is readily available, and
refuses to read Althusser's texts.

In recognition of Althusser's extremely controversial reputation, Derrida
read a statement at his funeral that accurately describes his achievement and
his protean elusiveness: "[Althusser] traversed so many lives . . . so many
personal, historical, philosophical and political adventures; marked, inflected,
influenced so many discourses, actions, and existences by the radiant and
provocative force of his thought, his manner of being, of speaking, of teaching,
that the most diverse and contradictory accounts could never exhaust their
source."[4] A persistent project that ran through the adventures of Althusser's
life was his determination to read Marx with the same kind of careful attention
to what Marx had actually written that Lacan had devoted to the texts of
Freud.[5] Thus, in a letter to Lacan, Althusser wrote, "You are . . . the first
thinker to assume the theoretical responsibility of giving Freud the real
concepts he deserves. . . . It was at the point where I realized that I was capable
of giving Marx's thought . . . its *theoretical form*, that I found myself on the
threshold of understanding you."[6] Althusser's choice of words here is quite
revealing: He credits Lacan with "giving" Freud the real concepts he deserves
and realizes that he himself is capable of "giving" Marx's thought its theoretical form. In his return to the texts of Freud, Lacan had not only worked to
recover Freud's thought from its appropriation by the various psychoanalytic
associations throughout the world that had been founded to preserve it and
from the many popularizations of Freudianism; he was also determined to turn
Freud's own critical procedures back on what Freud had written in order to
save Freud from himself.[7] For Lacan this meant a careful study of Freud's
poetics (his argument by metaphor and his rhetoric of allusion); an attentive-
ness to the trajectory of Freud's thought, even when his arguments were
incomplete or malformed; and a willingness to reject what Freud wrote when
it seemed in a given instance to contradict what he had written more impor-
tantly elsewhere.

As ambitious as Lacan's project was, Althusser's was even more so. Marx's
texts have not yet been completely edited and translated into French and
English with the degree of care that has been lavished on Freud's writings.
(Modern editors of Marx's *Complete Works*, which in English is expected to
reach 50 volumes, obviously do not have James Strachey's advantage of being
able to consult with Marx about textual difficulties.) Furthermore, the intellectual significance and political enactment of Marx's thought is unprec-

edented in modern times. What Althusser faced in his determination to read Marx was the necessity of recovering Marx's thought from its many appropriations (from Engels and Lenin to Stalinism and the French Communist Party) and from its popular journalistic misrepresentations and denunciations.[8] Furthermore, Althusser had to deal with Marx as a writer of many different kinds of texts: some of them as a coauthor with Engels, such as *The German Ideology*; some of them aphoristic, such as the "Theses on Feuerbach"; some of them occasional pieces in the form of letters or newspaper articles; some of them careful historical studies, such as *The Eighteenth Brumaire of Louis Bonaparte*; some of them polemically rhetorical, such as the *Manifesto of the Communist Party*; and some of them highly experimental, detailed theoretical texts, such as *Capital*.[9]

Althusser does not propose to read Marx's texts sequentially, but because he does devote considerable effort to locating the "epistemological break" in Marx's thought in 1846 with the publication of *The German Ideology*, which separates the "ideological" from the "scientific" writings,[10] a preliminary sense of the chronology of Marx's early writing is useful for understanding Althusser's project.[11] Marx's first publications were journalistic articles, several of which were written in opposition to censorship laws, arguing that, like slavery, censorship can never be justified. Marx thought it an illusion to believe that the state has a will that can rightfully be opposed to independent, particular interests. Similarly in the *Critique of Hegel's Philosophy of Right* and his essay *On the Jewish Question*, Marx advocated human emancipation through an identification of private with public life and the idea that the individual carries forward the essence of the community. In the introduction to the *Critique of Hegel's Philosophy of Right*, Marx sets forth for the first time the two related ideas that the proletariat has a historical mission and that revolution is a fulfillment of the innate dynamics of history.

In 1844 Marx was in Paris, where he devoted himself to writing a critique of political economy that would become the foundation of *Capital*. *The Economic and Philosophical Manuscripts of 1844*, which were not published until 1932, absorb and transcend Hegel's concept of alienation with the argument that the condition of labor has become the principal source of alienation in the modern world. Here the conflict is between two views of human essence: For Hegel it is self-consciousness, while for Marx it is labor, by which human beings externalize themselves and impact on nature. It appears to have been his reading of Feuerbach that led Marx to see the limitations of Hegel's philosophy. The "Theses on Feuerbach," a series of aphorisms that were written in 1845 and published in 1888 by Engels after Marx's death, include nonetheless Marx's fundamental opposition to Feuerbach's theory of knowledge, his religious views, and his concept of human beings. For Marx, knowledge, which is a practical not just a contemplative matter, concerns itself with what is real, actual, and sensuous. Thus it is a fatal error to deal with religion or human essence as Feuerbach had done, apart from the totality of social relationships. In this context Marx's famous but commonly misunderstood thesis that "the philosophers have only *interpreted* the world differently; the point, however, is to *change* it" (GI, 199), is a criticism of abstract German philosophical idealism in the Hegelian tradition and not a rejection of philosophy as a whole in favor of uninformed social action. Although Marx does not employ this language with absolute consistency even after 1846, the word "ideology" is used here to signify abstract idealism, and the word "science" to signify knowledge based upon and thoroughly engaged in historically informed social action. Whether or under what circumstances science emerges from ideology is a persistent problem in Marx's thought that Althusser rightly sees as basic to an understanding of what Marx wrote. Nevertheless, Engels's *The Situation of the Working Class in England* (1845), which was published the year after his 40-year friendship and collaboration with Marx began, seemed to be exactly the kind of informed, detailed, meticulous account of the specific conditions of starvation, poverty, and alienation that Marx believed would redirect the production of knowledge and help change the world. But for such change to be possible, the ideology of philosophical idealism, which distorted and concealed social reality, needed to be critically exposed.

The first books to come out of the collaboration between Marx and Engels were *The Holy Family*, a biting and mocking denunciation of the Young Hegelians with whom Marx had associated in Bonn and Cologne, and *The German Ideology*, which was to be a key text for Althusser. The opening sentences of *The German Ideology* are simultaneously a lucid statement of the plan of the book, an announcement of the project that would occupy Marx and Engels for the rest of their lives, and the foundation for a critical understanding of ideology:

> Hitherto men have constantly made up for themselves false conceptions about themselves, about what they are and what they ought to be. They have arranged their relationships according to ideas of God, of normal man, etc. The phantoms of their brains have gained the mastery over them. They, the creators, have bowed down before their creatures. Let us liberate them from the chimeras, the ideas, dogmas, imaginary beings under the yoke of which they are pining away. (GI, 1)

Although, in his eulogy for Marx, Engels lists the critique of ideology along with the concept of surplus value as constituting Marx's most important contribution to knowledge (SW, 411), neither Marx nor Engels developed a systematic theory of ideology, despite several important scattered references to the concept (SW, 344–5, 577, 582, 656, 659–60).[12] Assuming that Engels's letter of July 14, 1893 to Franz Mehring grasps the essence of the concept, ideology is a condition of false consciousness that is mistaken for true thought or for knowledge of the forces that determine thought.[13] While in the grip of ideology, the thinker is unaware that his or her ideas concerning philosophy, religion, history, economics, politics, law are actually the products of social interests and conditions that are independent of thought (SW, 659). Ultimately, what ideology works to conceal is that the conflicts of material life are what actually determine thought; or, in the succinct language of *The German Ideology*, "Life is not determined by consciousness, but consciousness by life" (GI, 15). Later, in the preface to *A Contribution to the Critique of Political Economy*, Marx developed this insight into a passage that brilliantly captures the essence of his understanding of political economy:

> [T]he guiding principle of my studies can be summarised as follows. In the social production of their existence, men inevitably enter into definite relations, which are independent of their will, namely relations of production appropriate to a given stage in the development of their material forces of production. The totality of these relations of production constitutes the economic structure of society, the real foundation, on which arises a legal and political superstructure and to which correspond definite forms of social consciousness. The mode of production of material life conditions the general process of social, political, intellectual life. It is not the consciousness of men that determines their existence, but their social existence that determines their consciousness. (SW, 173)

Because of their sense of the role of the Young Hegelians in the construction of German ideology, Marx and Engels saw the intellectual as the most likely ideologist in that he deceives himself by thinking of his ideas as free and true, rather than critically reflecting on them as the product of his social situation. All philosophers, religious thinkers, jurists, social reformers, and political innovators are (they claim) particularly vulnerable to the false consciousness of ideology, which only knowledge based on a systematic critique of political economy can expose.

Unlike Feuerbach, however, Marx and Engels believed that philosophy alone could not expose and counter ideology. They were convinced that the social conditions that produced ideology needed to be radically changed if human beings were to be freed from false consciousness. Marx's continuing quarrel with Feuerbach was basically that he did not see the necessity of turning critical philosophy into social action, which Marx and Engels believed was essential in order to end alienation, to make productive human happiness possible, and to replace ideology with knowledge. As Engels put it in *Feuerbach and the End of Classical German Philosophy* (1888), "The great basic question of all, especially of latter-day, philosophy, is that concerning the relation of thinking and being" (SW, 568). No doubt the most important question to ask of Althusser's work, then, is whether his commitment to reading Marx the way he does contributes to that relation or whether it is an unwitting return to Feuerbach.[14] But whatever one's final judgment of Althusser's work, there seems to be no alternative to basing that judgment on a careful reading of what he wrote. Here "Ideology and Ideological State Apparatuses" (1969) is the appropriate starting point.[15]

Although that text has the subtitle "Notes Towards an Investigation," it is nevertheless a very systematic and carefully structured piece of writing. The argument is divided into five unnumbered sections, each with a title in vertical type; the subdivisions of these sections are indicated by titles in italics; and there is an untitled postscript at the end, which is dated 1970.[16] The ostensible occasion for the entire text is an effort to answer a question that arises from reading Marx's letter to Kugelmann (July 11, 1868): What (in Marx's thought and in the world of political economy) is the reproduction of the means of production that is necessary for production to continue (127)? The obvious answer to this question, as the "average" economist and capitalist well know, is that raw materials and machinery need to be replenished and serviced to make continued production possible (129). But there is also a subtler answer, which requires considerable effort in order to bring forward for critical examination what is usually an unexamined part of the structure of everyday consciousness. Once that effort is made and the necessity of renewing labor power as a means of reproduction becomes clear (130), then a whole set of other necessities is revealed, including the laborers' wages and education. As a condition of the reproduction of the means of production, education is a means of imparting the rules of good capitalist behavior: "i.e. the attitude that should be observed by every agent in the division of labour, according to the job he is 'destined' for: rules of morality, civic and professional conscience, which actually means rules of respect for the socio-technical division of labour and ultimately the rules of the order estab-lished by class domination" (132). Thus, a large portion of the "know-how" that is taught to children in capitalist societies ensures "subjection to the ruling ideology" (133) of the capitalist state. The *sine qua non* of the reproduc-tion of labor power is, then, its subjection to the practice of the state ideologi-cal apparatuses (133).

Already this unmasking of the role of ideology in capitalist production leads to a second question, "What is a society?" (134). Just as Freud conceived the structure of the mind as consisting of discrete levels or localizations, so Marx distinguished between the infrastructure or economic base and the two levels of social superstructure, the politico-legal and the ideological. An important text for Althusser in drawing these distinctions would seem to be a brief passage in Marx's preface to *The Critique of Political Economy*:

> Changes in the economic foundation lead sooner or later to the transformation of the whole immense superstructure. In studying such transformations it is always necessary to distinguish between the material transformation of the economic conditions of production, which can be determined with the precision of natural science, and the legal, political, religious, artistic or philosophic – in short, ideological forms in which men become conscious of [the conflict between the material productive forces and the existing relations of production] and fight it out. (SW, 174)

The principal thing to be noticed in such passages as this, Althusser argues, is that base and superstructure are metaphorical elements in the theory and that the object of this metaphor of the edifice is to represent the ultimate determining powers of the economic base. Like all conceptual metaphors, however, this one is approximate and unstable. For example, the "place" of ideology in this metaphor keeps shifting. If the structure of the state includes a base or infrastructure (say, level 1) consisting of the reproduction of the conditions of production (1a) and production itself (1b), and a superstructure (say, level 2) consisting of the politico-legal superstructure (2a) and of ideology (2b), then ideology functions simultaneously on level 1a and 2b. This implies both the relative autonomy of the superstructure and the "reciprocal action of the superstructure on the base" (136).

Despite the necessary approximation and relative instability of Marx's theoretical language, what is particularly fascinating here for Althusser is Marx's effort to see his theory through its first or descriptive phase (138), which is analogous to Freud's wrestling with his two models for the structure of the mind (conscious–unconscious and id–ego–superego) and his elaborate archaeological metaphors for mental history.[17] Marx's epistemological ambition is nothing less than a determination to construct a theory to account for the complex processes of state power, which affect all aspects of human life. In his careful studies of the brief history of the Paris Commune of 1871, for example, Marx had come to an understanding of the inherently repressive force of state power: "After every revolution marking a progressive phase in the class struggle, the purely repressive character of the State power stands out in bolder and bolder relief," he wrote gloomily in *The Civil War in France* (SW, 272). Even after the working class had seized control of "the old state machine," it continued to be a repressive mechanism. On the occasion of the twentieth anniversary of the Commune, Engels makes this point with brilliant clarity and conciseness:

> What had been the characteristic attribute of the former state? Society had created its own organs to look after its common interests, originally through simple division of labour. But these organs, at whose head was the state power, had in the course of time, in pursuance of their own special interests, trans- formed themselves from the servants of society into the masters of society. (SW, 245)

Although this insight is fundamental to what Marx had written in *The Eighteenth Brumaire of Louis Bonaparte* (especially SW, 165–8) and in *The Civil War in France* – where his account of the Paris Commune is introduced by the sentence. "The working class cannot simply lay hold of the ready-made State machinery, and wield it for its own purposes" (SW, 272) – he was, neverthe- less, far too quick to assume that the repressive powers of ideological institu- tions could be definitively swept away. For example, he writes as follows about the Commune's work to "break the spiritual force of oppression":

> The whole of the educational institutions were opened to the people gratui- tously, and at the same time cleared of all interference of Church and State. Thus, not only was education made accessible to all, but science itself freed from the fetters which class prejudice and governmental force had imposed upon it. (SW, 274)

Here the development of Marx's theory of ideology had fallen behind his understanding of what Althusser calls the Repressive State Apparatuses, but his lapse is precisely the opening for Althusser's addition to classical Marxism. What he adds, however, as he candidly admits (141), was in a sense already there in Marx and Engels's earlier nascent theory of ideology.

Althusser generously acknowledges (142n) the importance of Antonio Gramsci's earlier recognition that the power of the state is not confined to the Repressive State Apparatus. Indeed, it is as though Althusser is here reading Marx through a lens provided by Gramsci's *Prison Notebooks*. There, the key passage for Althusser seems to be the climax of Gramsci's distinction between the state and civil society, a distinction that is also implicit in such texts by Marx as *The Eighteenth Brumaire of Louis Bonaparte* and *The Class Struggles in France 1848–1850*. Both Gramsci and Althusser are very much aware of the complexities of the textual genealogies they have inherited. At the risk of oversimplification, these may be outlined as follows: For both Gramsci and Althusser, Hegel's conception of the state constitutes the first generation of ideas, not only because Marx and Althusser were profoundly influenced by Hegel (which both of them tried to conceal),[18] but also because, as a contemporary of the French Revolution, Hegel (according to Gramsci) believed in the limitless spread of the bourgeoisie and in the eventual achievement of an ethical state.[19] Marx and Engels's understanding of the tenaciously repressive machinery of the state constitutes the second generation of ideas. Marx had witnessed Hegel's thought reaching a static impasse as it passed into the writings of Feuerbach, but he also had the advantage of seeing more clearly than Hegel the aftermath of the French Revolution of 1789 and of witnessing and chronicling the civil wars in France, beginning in 1848. Gramsci's explanation that the working class did not carry out its revolutionary mission that Marx had envisioned – because of the control of ideology by the ruling class – constitutes the third generation of texts for Althusser. Finally, Althusser, as though in a fourth generation, looks back through this legacy of commentary, prophecy, and disappointment in an effort to read Marx carefully and critically through it.[20]

It is not surprising that, as the power of the state is reassessed from Hegel and Marx to Gramsci and Althusser, the language of the relevant texts changes as the political theory evolves. Marx, for example, distinguishes between the state and civil society (e.g., SW, 102); Gramsci, following Croce, distinguishes between the political state and the ethical or cultural state; and Althusser works to distinguish between the Repressive State Apparatuses and the Ideological State Apparatuses. The passage in Gramsci that seems to have been most important for Althusser's project is this:

> In my opinion, the most reasonable and concrete thing that can be said about the ethical State, the cultural State, is this: every State is ethical in as much as one of its most important functions is to raise the great mass of the population to a particular cultural and moral level, a level (or type) which corresponds to the needs of the productive forces for development, and hence to the interests of the ruling classes. The school as a positive educative function, and the courts as a repressive and negative educative function, are the most important State activities in this sense: but, in reality, a multitude of other so-called private initiatives and activities tend to the same end – initiatives and activities which form the apparatus of the political and cultural hegemony of the ruling classes.[21]

As a development of Marx's concept of civil society and Gramsci's of the ethical or cultural state, Althusser's Ideological State Apparatuses finally defy the distinction between public and private (144) and between repressive and non-repressive (145). For Althusser all ideology is in some sense repressive, and all state apparatuses are in some sense ideological. But as ideology works non-violently and in some sense with the complicity of the repressed, it unifies the various institutional manifestations of the ideological state apparatuses, which include religion, the schools, the family, the law, political parties, the trade unions, communication media, and such cultural instruments as litera-ture, the arts, and sports (143). Citing a passage from Marx's preface to *A Contribution to the Critique of Political Economy*, Althusser argues that although the class struggle extends beyond ideology, it is through a critical understand-ing of ideology that people become conscious of class conflict and acquire the means of turning ideology back against the classes in power (147n).

Section 4 of Althusser's text returns to a reworded version of the question with which he bagan – "how is the reproduction of the relations of production secured?" (148) – and summarizes his argument that for the most part it is secured by the Ideological State Apparatuses, especially by the "educational ideological apparatus" (152). Althusser claims that the principal achievement of the French Revolution was its attack on the Church, which at the time was the primary Ideological State Apparatus; but since the Revolution, the school has replaced the Church, in its pact with the family, as the most powerful ideological source. Here Althusser develops a musical metaphor to account for the way the influence of the school is woven among other ideological agencies. It is as though the school provides an ideological score containing such "great themes" as classical humanism, the "miracle" of pre-Christian Greek civiliza-tion, the glories of Rome as the Eternal City, and the rise of European nationalism, which are then performed in concert by the other Ideological State Apparatuses (154–5). Although a few exceptional teachers, each of whom is "a kind of hero," manage to teach against the ideological system in which they are trapped, most teachers persist in the illusion that the school is ideologically neutral, that the free consciences of the students are being respected, and that they are being taught virtues that are liberating and responsible (156–7).

The final section of "Ideology and Ideological State Apparatuses" carries out a survey of Marx's scattered observations about ideology and develops an analogy between the status of dream experience in Freudian theory and ideol-ogy as an imaginary construction in classical Marxism. Because ideology is "pure illusion," it has no history, although particular ideologies (such as the Church or the school) do. Like dream experience, ideology is an *assemblage* (cf. Deleuze), a *bricolage* (cf. Lévi-Strauss and Derrida), or a residue of daily ex-perience (160). Although particular ideologies rise and fall, ideology as a shadow of knowledge, like the unconscious, is eternal (161). But the greatest and most insidious power of ideology, according to Althusser, is its capacity to represent to human beings an imaginary conception of their own subjectivity. Although Althusser does not here mention Lacan by name, both his understanding of Freud and his comments on the imaginary construction of human subjects are heavily indebted to Lacan's paper on "The Mirror State."[22] Here, in the final section of "Ideology and Ideological State Apparatuses," Althusser works to close the gap between Freud's and Marx's conceptions of alienation, which for him is a person's realization that she or he cannot become the fully individuated, autonomous subject projected by the image promoted by educational ideology and reinforced by the family. While promising to liberate the subject, the educational ideological apparatus makes human beings in fact subject to a force in the state more tenacious than any component of the Repressive State Apparatus. Althusser concludes with the candid admission that his theory of ideology (like Marx's) is incomplete. Both the *"total process* of the realization of the reproduction of the relations of production" (183) and "the class nature of the ideologies existing in a social formation" (184) need to be explained. What Althusser achieved in this paper, however, is a systematic articulation of one of Marx's two most important contributions to knowledge. The other contribution, based on the theory of surplus value, is the subject of Althusser's *Reading Capital*.

NOTES

1 Paul Ricoeur, *Lectures on Ideology and Utopia*, ed. George H. Taylor (New York: Columbia University Press, 1986); Fredric Jameson, *The Political Unconscious* (Ithaca, NY: Cornell Unversity Press, 1981); E. P. Thompson, *The Poverty of Theory and Other Essays* (New York: Monthly Review Press, 1978).

2 Louis Althusser, *The Future Lasts Forever: A Memoir*, trans. Richard Veasey (New York: New Press, 1993). The best account of these autobiographical texts is Gregory Elliott, "Analysis Terminated, Analysis Interminable: The Case of Louis Althusser," in *Althusser: A Critical Reader* (Oxford: Blackwell, 1994), pp. 177–202. Elliott is also preparing an intellectual biography of Althusser.

3 Geraldine Finn, *Why Althusser Killed His Wife* (Atlantic Highlands, NJ: Humanities Press, 1996), pp. 5, 71. The title essay was first published in *Canadian Forum*, 61 (September–October 1981), 28–9.

4 Jacques Derrida, "Louis Althusser," in E. Ann Kaplan and Michael Sprinker (eds), *The Althusserian Legacy* (London: Verso, 1993), p. 27. In *Specters of Marx*, (trans. Peggy Kamuf [London: Routledge, 1994], pp. 89–90) Derrida distinguishes his approach to Marx from Althusser's.

5   Cf. David Macey, "Thinking with Borrowed Concepts: Althusser and Lacan," in *Althusser: A Critical Reader* (Oxford: Blackwell, 1994), pp. 142–58.

6   Quoted by Macey, p. 143.

7   For a detailed account of Lacan's readings of Freud, see my *Reading Theory* (Oxford: Blackwell, 1993), ch. 2.

8   Even such a basically sympathetic study of Marx as Joan Robinson's *An Essay on Marxian Economics* (London: Macmillan. 1942) sets out to extract Marx's argument from what she supposes to be the "obscurities in his theory," the crudeness of his intellectual tools, and the pecularity of his language (pp. v, 2, 4). It is not surprising that Robinson ignores the importance of ideology in Marx's thought. For an account of French Marxism before Althusser, see George Lichtheim, *Marxism in Modern France* (New York: Columbia University Press, 1966), pp. 86–108, and David Caute, *Communism and the French Intellectuals, 1914–1960* (London: Macmillan, 1964), pp. 263–80. Derrida provides a brief but important critique of Kojève's influence on French Marxism in *Specters of Marx*, pp. 91–4.

9   All citations from Marx and Engels's writings, unless otherwise noted, are to the *Complete Works* (London: Lawrence and Wishart). The following abbreviations are used with page numbers in parentheses: GI for *The German Ideology* (which includes the posthumously published "Theses on Feuerbach") and SW for the *Selected Works of Marx and Engels*.

10   *For Marx*, trans. Ben Brewster (New York: Pantheon, 1969), p. 34.

11   For this chronology I follow Leszek Kolakowski, *Main Currents of Marxism: Its Rise, Growth, and Dissolution*, trans. P. S. Falla, 3 vols (Oxford: Clarendon Press, 1978), even though Kolakowski's brief comment on Althusser (vol. III, pp. 483–6) is not reliable. To my knowledge, the best one-volume study of Marx in English is still David McLellen, *Karl Marx: His Life and Thought* (London: Macmillan, 1973). Althusser devotes a considerable portion of the introduction to *For Marx* to establishing a chronology and periodization of Marx's thought (pp. 31–8).

12   Cf. Bhikhu Parakh, *Marx's Theory of Ideology* (Baltimore: Johns Hopkins University Press, 1982), esp. pp. 136–63.

13   The best brief history of ideology as term and concept is Raymond Williams, *Keywords: A Vocabulary of Culture and Society* (New York: Oxford University Press, 1976), pp. 126–30.

14   See Louis Althusser, "Philosophy as a Revolutionary Weapon," in *Lenin and Philosophy and Other Essays*, trans. Ben Brewster (New York: Monthly Review Press, 1971), pp. 11–22: "In 1948, when I was 30, I became a teacher of philosophy and joined the PCF [the French Communist Party]. Philosophy was an interest; I was trying to make it my profession. Politics was a passion; I was trying to become a Communist militant. My interest in philosophy was aroused by materialism and its critical function: for *scientific* knowledge, against all the mystifications of *ideological* 'knowledge'" (p. 11). Althusser is quite right, how-

ever, in his emphasis on the hold of Feuerbach's thought on Marx until 1845 (*For Marx*, pp. 44–5).

15   For a bibliography of Althusser's published writings, see Gregory Elliott (ed.), *Althusser: A Critical Reader*, pp. 203–14. A considerable amount of important material, which is deposited in the archives of the Institut Mémoires de l'Édition Contemporaine in Paris, is still unpublished.

16   "Ideology and Ideological State Apparatuses," in *Lenin and Philosophy*, pp. 127–86, referred to hereafter by page numbers in parentheses. The divisions of the text are as follows: Section 1 (pp. 127–34), 1a (pp. 128–30), 1b (pp. 130–4); Section 2 (pp. 134–6); Section 3 (pp. 137–48), 3a (pp. 138–40), 3b (pp. 140–1), 3c (pp. 141–8); Section 4 (pp. 148–57); Section 5 (pp. 158–83), 5a (pp. 159–62), 5b (pp. 162–70), 5c (pp. 170–7), 5d (pp. 177–83); PS (pp. 183–6).

17   Cf. Malcolm Bowie, *Freud, Proust and Lacan: Theory as Fiction* (Cambridge: Cambridge University Press, 1987).

18   See, for example, *For Marx*, pp. 35–6, 223–4.

19   Antonio Gramsci, *Selections from the Prison Notebooks*, trans. Quintin Hoare and Geoffrey Nowell Smith (New York: International Publishers, 1971), pp. 258–9.

20   Althusser in turn subjected his own work to a severe critical reading, both in *Éléments d'autocritique* (Paris: Hachette, 1974) and in *The Future Lasts Forever*.

21   Gramsci, *Prison Notebooks*, p. 258.

22   This paper is discussed in detail below in chapter 8.

4

Foucault's The Order of Things: An Archaeology of the Human Sciences

In "Nietzsche, Genealogy, History" Foucault was highly suspicious of historical investigations that attempt to determine what things are by positing their origin or their emergent outcome. Many recent assessments of Foucault's work, however, have not hesitated to designate such terminal points in his thought. For example. Arnold Davidson, in a highly influential essay, has argued that there are three successive emphases in Foucault's work: his analyses of systems of knowledge, modalities of power, and the self's relation to itself. Each of these emphases might be thought to require specific forms of analysis: archaeology (the investigation of truth as a system of procedures governing forms of discourse): genealogy (a focus on the mutual relations between systems of truth and modalities of power); and ethics (a study of the self's relationship to itself, or "how the individual is supposed to constitute himself as a moral subject of his own actions").[1] Although this scheme is helpful in clarifying Foucault's project and in simplifying the order of his hundreds of publications, the sequence of his thought is more complex than this: Investigations of modalities of power/knowledge are very much a part of his discourse analyses, and his ethical project subsumes both of these. All three emphases and methods of analysis are present in *The Order of Things*.

Alan Sheridan's excellent English translation of *Les Mots et les choses: une archéologie des sciences humaines* (1966) restored to Foucault's most influential text the title he had originally preferred.[2] In both its French and English versions *The Order of Things* is divided into ten chapters, which are grouped in two parts: 1 to 6 and 7 to 10. The first six deal with the historical and social determinations of knowledge, and the last four – while not abandoning those earlier categories – question their adequacy by subjecting them in turn to the kind of critique they themselves make possible. The first and most famous chapter, which is an elegant essay on Velázquez's painting *Las Meninas*, was added to the manuscript in response to Pierre Nora's fortunate judgment that it is an appropriately seductive preface to the book as a whole, a preface that Foucault, however, at first thought too literary.[3] *The Order of Things* is nothing less than a history of systems of knowledge from the Renaissance to the modern age (roughly from the sixteenth to the mid-twentieth century). Foucault's concern was not just with what was known during those times, but more specifically with what constituted knowledge during each of three epochs, as they are commonly distinguished in France: the Renaissance (the sixteenth to the mid-seventeenth century), the Classical Age (from the mid-seventeenth century to the end of the eighteenth century), and the Modern Age (from the eighteenth century to approximately the time Foucault was writing: slightly past the middle of the twentieth century).

Each of these historical periods produced its particular configuration of knowledge, which Foucault calls an "episteme." This he defines elsewhere as "all those relationships which existed between the various sectors of science during a given epoch."[4] Strictly speaking, then, there is only one governing episteme for a given epoch (168). Epistemes both enable and limit the production of knowledge, not simply by external, institutional, or political manipulation but by their own determination of the extent of possible intellectual production. In this sense, they are charged simultaneously by both intellectual and cultural power, although they are not as absolute as Kantian categories nor as institutionally specific as Kuhnian paradigms. Most simply put, the three epistemes during the periods that concern Foucault are "the knowledge of living beings, the knowledge of the laws of language, and the knowledge of economic facts" (x). He proposes to set these epistemes "side by side" and to relate them to the philosophical discourses that were contemporary with them. This procedure has two consequences: It destabilizes facile connections between a given century or epoch and the origins or emergence of a given science; and it reveals a network of analogies among the epistemes. Foucault is not proposing that what constitutes knowledge at a given time is determined simply by social, political, economic, or similar constructs; rather, that these constructs are also themselves historically determined and that their limitations can be critically examined. Thus, he resists simply equating the emergence of linguistics or biology or economics with a given epoch when, for example, there were Port Royal grammarians, a Darwin, or a Marx; or with eras when the French Academy or Victorian imperialism or the European Industrial Revolution made powerful interventions into the production of knowledge. Indeed, what eventually became linguistics, biology, and economics is much more genealogically complex than the achievements of a single thinker, a limited group of thinkers, a single ideology, or a social movement. Even more important, Foucault observes that some of the most significant advances in knowledge have occurred when, by "analogies among the epistemes," a given science breaks out from its restrictive confines – refusing, for example, to determine truth by economic and political constructions alone – and forms a hybrid with another science. Accordingly, Foucault's mind reaches out to the visual arts, to literature, to history, and to philosophy no less than to the human sciences of linguistics, biology, and economics.

In what may now seem a rhetorically restrained project, Foucault was determined to resist any facile reductive moralizing or thoughtless political engagement, as though to manifest the conviction that political activity without critical reflection is simply a localized instance of totalitarianism or repressive ideology. Indeed, his meticulous investigations of the histories of asylums, prisons, and hospitals proved to have a legitimacy and political force that would have been unthinkable without their insistence on being carefully documented and true.[5] Like Habermas more recently, Foucault was determined to demonstrate that an intellectual's political efficacy rests solely on a foundation of scholarship.[6] Only in this respect is the power of knowledge politically legitimate.

Foucault invokes two metaphors for his analytical procedure: It is like excavating at an archaeological dig in which his text can be read as "an open site" (xii); and it is like conducting a psychoanalytic session that reveals the unconscious "rules" used by naturalists, economists, and grammarians to define their studies. In this sense his procedure is to be distinguished from traditional epistemological investigations of scientific consciousness (xiii) because he is dealing with unconscious or buried orders of knowledge. Although Foucault does not make this point explicitly, if his procedure is analogous to psychoanalysis, then his rendering of epistemes in his text might effect a "transference" response from his readers, in which they might find themselves symbolically implicated in his argument, as though the structures of knowledge that may have operated unconsciously in the reader's mind are the objects of his investigation. In other words, Foucault as a writer may be understood to have fashioned a style that enables him on one level to write about the power structures of knowledge, while on another level revealing his readers' complicity in maintaining those structures. (In a review essay entitled "Taking Sides," Barthes refers to Foucault's procedure as the asking of "a cathartic question" addressed to all of knowledge.)[7] Although Foucault emphasizes his archaeological more than his psychoanalytic metaphor, it is useful to recall that Freud's principal metaphor for psychoanalysis was that it is an archaeology of the mind, which unearths and deciphers previously lost or buried inscriptions.[8] Nevertheless, both archaeology and psychoanalysis are metaphors for Foucault; as sciences in their own right, they are not immune to the same kind of investigation he conducts into biology, linguistics, and economics. In his final chapter, Foucault turns his critical procedure onto psychoanalysis and ethnography, which might previously have seemed privileged disciplines.

As the subtitle of his book – *An Archaeology of the Human Sciences* – indicates, Foucault's goal is to inquire into the foundations of the human sciences. But in the surprising conclusion to his book, he wonders whether the concept of man might be washed away by the waves of history, like an image in the sand. Indeed, even in 1966, especially in the intellectual culture of which Foucault was part, "man" (*l'homme*) had already been replaced by "subject" (*le sujet*) in order to emphasize what Foucault calls "the problem of the subject" (xiii): Is man simply the construct of a particular moment in history and therefore vulnerable to the rise and fall of epistemes? If so, then man is a construction of those human sciences that Foucault has set out to excavate. Furthermore, the structures of discourse in the human sciences – especially in linguistics, biology, and economics – have had a determinative influence on the way modern knowledge – or the governing epistemes of the post-Enlightenment have been ordered. Foucault assumes that most of his readers operate unaware of but nevertheless profoundly under the influence of those orders, as though the orders are still intact without one's needing to think about them. Human beings are thus in danger of ordering things and themselves thoughtlessly. But Foucault sets out to enable his readers to reflect on how they are to remedy their thoughtlessness and question the adequacy of their epistemological habits and horizons.

In undertaking such an investigation, however, Foucault acknowledges that he is not only working a neglected field but also one that is suspect (ix). In contrast to the respectable regularity of histories of mathematics, cosmology, and physics, the histories of biology, linguistics, and economics are commonly thought to be irregular, their discourses contaminated by imagery, and their intellectual course subject to the vagaries of empirical chance. Against these suspicions, Foucault launches a succession of "What ifs": "What if empirical knowledge, at a given time and in a given culture, *did* possess a well-defined regularity?" What if the way facts get recorded were not at the mercy of chance, if even errors that are derived from ancient beliefs and pure naïveté obeyed certain epistemological laws, if suspect and informal knowledge itself had a history? What then? Although Foucault's book is driven by these questions, his method is comparative; thus he does not set out to epitomize his three historical periods (x). Rather, he juxtaposes the discourses of biology, linguistics, and economics with contemporaneous philosophical discourses from the seventeenth to the nineteenth centuries in order to reflect critically on those structures of knowledge and question customary divisions in historical time and epistemological territory that have become unquestioned because of their familiarity. What he works to uncover is a system of analogies (xi) among what are now established disciplines, and also the "epistemological space" that is distinctive in each particular historical period.

Following the foreword to the English edition, Foucault, in his preface, recalls a passage in which Borges describes a certain Chinese encyclopaedia in which animals are sorted into the following categories:

> (a) belonging to the Emperor, (b) embalmed, (c) tame, (d) suckling pigs, (e) sirens, (f) fabulous, (g) stray dogs, (h) included in the present classification, (i) frenzied, (j) innumerable, (k) drawn with a very fine camelhair brush, (l) *et cetera*, (m) having just broken the water pitcher, (n) that from a long way off look like flies. (xv)

The experience of reading this passage and the laugh it produced, Foucault confesses (xv), were what prompted him to write *The Order of Things*. What constitutes the charm of such another system of thought as this, Foucault observes, is that it exposes the limitations of our own means of ordering things. Ordinarily, however, we are not aware of the limitations that our episteme imposes upon us, until we encounter Eusthenes's list, Roussel's umbrella and sewing-machine on the operating table, aphasiac orderings, or Borges's Chinese encyclopaedia. In Borges's example there may also be, however, the seductive appeal of a "mythical homeland" of meticulously ordered space, which at first appears as a different, more appealing, and more substantial order of things. Here, however, Foucault anticipates Derrida's discussion of the European hallucination of the East and Edward Said's critical account of the Western invention of the Orient, both of which are Western constructions of strategically useful illusions of otherness, which are manufactured in order to deprecate one's own culture as much as to exploit another's.[9] The point of Foucault's archaeology of epistemes is not to prod his reader into a thoughtless attempt to abandon his own culture for an illusory otherness, but rather to develop an awareness that "there is nothing more tentative . . . than the process of establishing an order among things" (xix).

To account for this tentativeness, Foucault makes two sets of distinctions that serve to relate his subject matter to the method of his investigation. The first distinguishes between two senses of order. On the one hand, there is the order that is "given in things as their inner law, the hidden network that determines the way they confront one another"; but on the other hand there is order that "has no existence except in the grid created by a glance, an examination, a language." Only within this grid – "as though already there, waiting in silence for the moment of its expression" – does order manifest itself

(xx) ["et c'est seulement dans les cases blanches de ce quadrillage qu'il se manifeste en profondeur déjà là, attendant en silence le moment d'être énoncé" (MC, 11)]. Like Freud's dream work, Foucault's archaeology sets out to decode systems of order as they manifest themselves in perception, thought, and language in an effort to uncover order in its latency. In this respect, the project of *The Order of Things* recalls the haunting preface to Foucault's *Madness and Civilization: A History of Insanity in the Age of Reason:*

> We have yet to write the history of that other form of madness, by which men, in an act of sovereign reason, confine their neighbors, and communicate and recognize each other through the merciless language of non-madness; to define the moment of this conspiracy before it was permanently established in the realm of truth, before it was revived by the lyricism of protest. We must try to return, in history, to that zero point in the course of madness at which madness is an undifferentiated experience, a not yet divided experience of division itself.[10]

In his explorations of both madness and order Foucault is drawn by reason's capacity to think beyond itself and by its ability to mark "the caesura that establishes the distance between reason and non-reason."[11] The prefaces to *Madness and Civilization* and *The Order of Things* both respond to Kant's preface to *The Critique of Pure Reason*, where he declares that the peculiar characteristic of reason is that it leads the mind to questions that it can neither ignore nor answer.[12] Foucault, however, boldly brings Kant's critique of reason together with Freud's critique of the unconscious, thereby greatly reducing the extent of the unanswerable.

Having made his primary distinction between two kinds of order, Foucault needs a second set of distinctions for the purpose of anticipating his method of inquiry. (1) At one extremity of thought lie those cultural codes that – by their governance of language, perceptual schema, means of exchange, systems of value – establish the empirical orders of human life. (2) At the other extremity of thought lie scientific and philosophical theories and interpretations that "explain why order exists in general, what universal law it obeys, what principle can account for it, and why this particular order has been established and not some other" (xx). (3) Between the distant extremities of cultural order and philosophical order is the pure experience of order itself. Here it is possible (as when confronting Borges's Chinese encyclopaedia) to free oneself sufficiently from one's own cultural order so that one can critically reflect upon it and discover that it is not the only possible order. However confused, obscure, and imprecise this intermediary position is, it is not necessarily any more outside of culture than it is outside of thought. As an intermediary position, it is the place where the claims of culture and the claims of critical thought overlap, emancipating order from the grid of language, perception, and practice, while criticizing that grid and rendering it partially invalid. "Thus," Foucault concludes, "in every culture, between the use of what one might call the ordering codes and reflections upon order itself, there is the pure experience of order and of its modes of being" (xxi). This is the area Foucault proposes to investigate in the interests of determining "the order on the basis of which we think today" (xxii). His project is to explore the caesura that determines the distance and the point of contact between cultural and critical theory; or, as he puts it later in the book, he is in search of "thought re-apprehending itself at the root of its own history" (217).

Part 1 of *The Order of Things* stretches out the grid that Foucault describes in his foreword and preface. The vertical lines of the grid mark the three genealogical epochs that run from the Renaissance through the Classical and Enlightenment periods to the Modern age; and the horizontal lines cut through that chronology with three epistemes: the sign (language), function (life), and conflict (wealth or labor). The first of the six chapters in Part 1 opens the argument of the book by allowing Velázquez's *Las Meninas* to sound several themes that are to be developed more fully in what follows. These include *the problem of the gaze*, or how we look at things and they at us (the point here being the need to reflect upon the problematics of perception, which is what Velázquez's painting emphasizes); *the problem of representation* (the point here being that because "no gaze is stable" [5], representations are discontinuous with what they purport to represent, which again accentuates the importance of the critical and interpretive role of the spectator); *the problem of language in relation to the visual* (the point being that just as the title of the picture – *The Maids of Honor* – does not exhaust or define what the picture represents, so neither the verbal nor the visual order can be reduced to the terms of the other, thus keeping continuously open the relationship between the sign and the image); *the problem of centrality* (the point being that by locating the convergence of observations or gazes that are occurring in the painting at a point exterior to it, Velázquez makes his viewer reflect upon the connections and discontinuities between inside and outside, representation and the represented, the object and the viewer). Velázquez's *Las Meninas* can therefore be viewed as a metonymy for the obsession with representation during the Classical age and as a metaphor for the trajectory of modern thought, not only by the way it brings the ostensible observers of the painting into it in the form of the reflections of the two sovereigns in the mirror, but also by the way it equalizes their presence with the paintings on the same wall. For Foucault, the painting as a whole undertakes to represent representation in all of its elements, including its essential void: "the necessary disappearance of that which is its foundation – of the person it resembles and the person in whose eyes it is only a resemblance" (16).

In chapter 2 Foucault provides a discursive elaboration of the rhetoric of resemblance during the Renaissance, against which the eras that more directly concern him, the Classical and the Modern, reacted. Up until the end of the sixteenth century – it is characteristic of Foucault's genealogical method that he does not say precisely when – resemblance "played a constructive" role in Western knowledge (17). In carrying out its epistemological function, resemblance assumed a variety of rhetorical forms, including *convenientia* (or juxtaposition), *aemulatio* (or "convenience" from a distance, such as man as microcosm of the universe), *analogy* (such as the body as a "universal atlas"), *sympathy* (or sameness as assimilation, its twin being *antipathy*). Such is the power of resemblances and their articulations that the world comes to be seen as a world of signs, where *signatures* are the visible signs of similarities written on the world (26), producing a "great untroubled mirror in which depths things gazed at themselves and reflected their own images back to one another" (27). It is not surprising, therefore, that the Renaissance produced the sciences of hermeneutics and semiology, the first to interpret the meaning of signs and the second to discover the location, definition, and links between signs. According to this scheme, nature is trapped in a dark space between the layers of hermeneutics and semiology. Because "language contained its own inner principle of proliferation" (40), knowledge consisted largely of commentary, by which one form of language was related to another with no need to justify claims of truth by other means.

Chapter 3 traces the twists, turns, and breaks in the Renaissance episteme of resemblance. Because Don Quixote is "a true likeness of all the signs that he has traced from his book" (46), he is the *reductio ad absurdum* or "negative" of the Renaissance world. The Classical age, as in the thought of Descartes and Bacon, takes up the difficult task of establishing discontinuities, which gives rise to the question of the relation of thought to culture: "How is it that thought has a place in the space of the world?" (50). A more modest version of that question is: How are signs represented in the Classical age? The sign does not silently wait to be found and read; rather, "it can be constituted only by an act of knowing" (59). The sign is now no longer thought to be universal, independent of space and time; rather, the Renaissance notion of the sign's universality is replaced by the idea of its infinite dispersion or dissemination in space and time. In the Classical age the man-made sign becomes more valued than the natural sign. Thus the key feature of the Classical episteme is not its presumed goal of recovering "the ancient Word" presumed to have the power to unlock the secrets of the world, but rather its determination "to fabricate a language" that will make possible a calculation of the world. The sign, therefore, became the calculus of analysis and combination (63). Here the order of things is not what determines the relation of the sign to its content; rather, the idea of one thing and the idea of another (as for the Port-Royal logicians) establish a bond "inside knowledge" (63) ["il est, à l'intérieur de la connaissance, le lien établi entre l'idée d'une chose et l'idée d'une autre" (MC 78)]. As a result of this bond, signs are coextensive with thought itself, and any theory of signification is precluded (65). Once the sign is located in the interstices of thought, two dimensions of analysis open up: investigations into the antitheses or inversions of representation in "non-actual but simultaneous . . . comparisons," such as impressions, reminescences, imaginings, memories – all aspects of "the image in time" (69); and investigations of the resemblance between things before their reduction to order. In an allusion to Destutt de Tracy's foundational text *Éléments d'idéologie* (1801–15), Foucault observes that these dimensions of analysis came together in the eighteenth century to produce ideology. But for a general science of order to develop within the Classical episteme – in either form of analysis – a mathesis or universal algebra, and a taxonomia or a universal system of signs were needed. Here mathesis and taxonomia are to be distinguished from genesis, which is the "constitution of orders on the basis of empirical series" (73). A crude simpli-fication of Foucault's sense of what was at stake in the shift from the Renais-sance to the Classical episteme would be that the focal point of knowledge shifted from words to ideas, even though both epistemes were suspicious of the concept of empirical genesis.

In reading a book as concerned as this one is with how we order things, it is impossible not to be sensitive to the multiple ways Foucault's text orders its materials. The basic order of both the text and what it sets out to represent from its sources – the history of systems of thought since the Renaissance – is sequential or chronological. Foucault has a story to tell, a supreme fiction of sorts. But the movement, for example, from the Renaissance to the Classical age does not leave behind the earlier episteme but rather revises it, just as one cannot resist the recurring temptation to reread earlier sections of *The Order of Things* in light of later ones. To take but one instance of reverse or cumulative chronology, the brilliant paragraph on the concept of literature with which chapter 2 ends is both a culmination of that chapter and an anticipation of the chapter on the advent of the Classical age to follow. But part of the argument of that paragraph is that *whenever* the student of literature "is no longer interrogating [literature] at the level of what it says but only in its significant form" (44), literature is being thought of in terms of an unexamined earlier episteme. Epistemic regression is always possible, even though "literature is appearing more and more [in the Modern era] as that which must be thought." This seems to be why Foucault cuts through his genealogical progression not only with condensed formulations of the epistemes – in the form of provisional theories of signs, functions, and conflict – but also with persistent attention to the philosophical and political implications of his history. Thus, Foucault's former teacher George Canguilhem makes an exceptionally useful observation in his magisterial review of *The Order of Things* when he points to the significance of Foucault's use of Velázquez and Cervantes. The term *espagnolisme*, he says, accurately captures Foucault's cast of mind. *Espagnolisme* for Foucault, as for Stendhal, meant "hatred for preachiness and platitudes."[13] Perhaps the subtlest but most important of the several ordering principles in the book is its persistent attack on late twentieth-century moralism and platitudinousness.

Foucault's chapter 4 on "Speaking" responds to some of the same texts discussed in Derrida's *Of Grammatology*, which was published a year after *The Order of Things*. Those texts include Rousseau's *Essay on the Origin of Languages*, Condillac's *An Essay on the Origin of Human Knowledge*, Warburton's *The Divine Legation of Moses*, and Duclos's *Commentary on the Port-Royal Grammar*. During the Classical age, Foucault argues, language "is both pre-eminent and unobtrusive" (78) in that once it is conceived to be equivalent with thought, its all-consuming importance virtually eliminates any independent theoretical space in which it can be assessed. In contrast, however, to the Renaissance sense of language as endless commentary, during the Classical age language works from the inside of representation, duplicating itself and hollowing itself out ["A partir de l'âge classique, le langage se déploie à l'intérieur de la représentation et dans ce dédoublement d'elle-même qui la creuse" (MC, 93)]. Here the primary text (the word within the world, or more accurately, the word as the world) gives way to discourse, within which internal spaces, crevices, or hollows provide the necessary openings for commentary to evolve into criticism:

> When this discourse becomes in turn an object of language, it is not questioned as if it were saying something without saying it, as if it were a language enclosed upon itself; one no longer attempts to uncover the great enigmatic statement that lies hidden beneath its signs; one asks how it functions: what representations it designates, what elements it cuts out and removes, how it analyses and composes, what play of substitutions enables it to accomplish its role of representation. (79–80)

Although his textual metaphors differ slightly from Foucault's, it is not surprising, since they are working with many of the same Classical texts, that

Derrida's understanding of language, textuality, and commentary verifies Foucault's.[14] Despite Derrida's emphasis on writing and Foucault's on speaking, deconstruction and criticism, by responding to processes already at work in texts, question "language as if language was a pure function, a totality of mechanisms, a great autonomous play of signs; but at the same time . . . cannot fail to question it as to its truth or falsehood" (80). Whereas commentary halts in awe before the original text, criticism and deconstruction interrogate the images, order, and ends of its truth claims. Foucault, however, sees the argument between commentary and criticism as endless. Unlike all other signs, language has the capacity to analyze the successive order of representation, by which, for example, the beauty *of* or *within* the rose must be represented in discourse as coming either *before* or *after* it (82). The quest for a general, philosophical, or universal grammar, which engaged Condillac, Domergue, Sicard, Adam Smith, Thiébault, the Port-Royal logicians, and the Encyclopedists was therefore driven by a determination to understand the "reflective decompostion of thought" and the link between representation and reflection (83).

Unlike the preceding chapters of *The Order of Things*, chapter 5 on "Classifying" is overtly polemical in its opposition to the anachronistic mode of most current histories of science. The common story about the origin of the life sciences during the seventeenth and eighteenth centuries is that a new sense of curiosity was created by the invention of the microscope and that this was coupled with the effort to extend the techniques of experimentation and calculation that had developed in the physical sciences (for example, in the work of Galileo and Newton) to the implementation of rational models for the study of living beings. The findings from the voyages of Tournefort and Adanson and the debate between the Cartesian mechanists and such vitalists as Blumenbach and Diderot provided the context for the fundamental controversy over the possibility of classifying things. While Linnaeus believed that a single taxonomy could be developed for all of nature, Buffon was convinced that nature was too complex and various to submit to a single system. Hume, whom Foucault does not cite until the end of the chapter (162) and in a different context, was even more radically skeptical in thinking that the systems and laws of nature created by science are not *in* nature but that they are simply patterns of order that suit the structures of human consciousness. According to the common story of the history of science that Foucault narrates, there are two emergent outcomes from the extension of rationality and the debates it created when applied to living beings: First, an irreversible and continuing conflict erupted between theological accounts of the hidden form and purpose beneath the observable elements of Creation and scientific accounts of natural autonomy. Second, there was a contradiction between scientific practice modelled on astronomy, mechanics, and optics, which assumed the immobility of nature and the practice of a new science that dealt with the creative, plastic, transformative powers of life, which includes human beings. What makes this story anachronistic, according to Foucault, is that, in its neglect of genealogy for origin and outcome, it looks at scientific practice in the Classical age in anticipation of the nineteenth-century theory of evolution, long before Darwin and Lamarck. Not only was natural selection as yet untheorized, but also biology as a science was unknown because the concept of life had not yet developed from the "grid of knowledge" (128) ["grille du savoir" (MC, 139)] about living beings that then constituted natural history.

When natural histories began to appear – Foucault gives 1657, the publication date of Jonston's *Natural History of Quadrupeds*, as an admittedly arbitrary date – a separation had begun to occur between two orders of historical knowledge. Whereas previously historians of plants and animals, such as Aldrovandi (in his *History of Serpents and Dragons*), wove together observation and fable, once signs became modes of representation in the Classical age, "what we see, what others have observed and handed down, and what others imagine" became distinguishable as observation, document, and fable (129). The appearance of natural histories, then, is part of a change in what constitutes history. No longer the indiscriminate compilation of everything documented, which simply waits to be retold by the chronicler, history took on a new meaning in the Classical age: "that of undertaking a meticulous examination of things themselves . . . and then of transcribing what it has gathered in smoothly neutralized and faithful words" (131). But to classify things in this way also required the concepts of structure and character and the distinction between continuity and catastrophe. Whereas structure "is that designation of the visible . . . by means of a kind of pre-linguistic sifting, [enabling] it to be transcribed into language" (138), character is a systematic selection of characteristics "whose variations and constants may be studied in any individual entity that presents itself" (139). Both structure and character presuppose a continuity in nature so strong as to accommodate change. Here Foucault aptly cites Charles Bonnet's *Palingénésie philosophique* (1770): "There will be a continual and more or less slow progress of all the species towards a superior perfection, with the result that all the degrees of the scale will be continually variable within a determined and constant relation" (151). Despite its significant achievements, natural history was decidedly limited not just to language but to a determination to give everything its proper name. Both the theory of nature and the theory of language during the Classical age left the assumption of resemblance intact.

Chapter 6, "Exchanging," begins with the observation that just as natural history and general grammar occupied the roles in the formation of knowledge that would later be assumed by biology and linguistics, so the study of wealth took the place of what would later be political economy. Foucault is not suggesting here that speaking, classifying, and exchanging are simply primitive forms of knowledge that later matured into the true sciences of the Modern era. Instead, these activities, when understood genealogically in terms of their historical possibilities and limitations continue to function as the enabling (and defining) foundation of modern knowledge. Foucault, however, repeatedly warns against thinking of the epistemes retrospectively (166), as though, for example, various fragments of political economy were at last gathered together in Adam Smith's understanding of division of labor, Ricardo's of capital, and Say's of the laws of market economy. In order to understand money, prices, value, and trade, it is necessary to turn to the analysis of wealth in the Classical age and not to anticipations of political economy as it came to be understood in the nineteenth century. It is in this context that Foucault makes the important observation that "In any given culture and at any given moment, there is always only one episteme that defines the conditions of possibility of all knowledge, whether expressed in a theory or silently invested in a practice" (168). Because of its link to practices and institutions, the analysis of wealth often works silently.

During the sixteenth century, various efforts were made throughout Europe to standardize the value of money, in France, for example, by establishing the gold écu as both a real coin and an accounting unit. But "the sign the coins bore – the *valor impositus* – was merely the exact and transparent mark of the measure they constituted" (170). Despite these efforts to fix the signification or value of money, the fact of *re*-standardization and the recognition that coins with a high percentage of metal are more likely to be hoarded than circulated (Gresham's law), it eventually became clear that money is a commodity like any other (171). In short, sixteenth-century practices concerning money were determined by signs constituted by resemblances that required commentary (or further signs) in order to be known (172). In the Classical age, this Renaissance configuration dissolved and was replaced by the exchange function of coinage. An important consequence of this move is the expansion of the concept of wealth to encompass all representable objects of desire that are marked, according to the formulation of Grammont, by "necessity, or utility, or pleasure, or rarity" (175). Thus, the relation of money to wealth becomes arbitrary (176); money is the sign that enables wealth to be represented (177); the relationships between the two, because goods multiply when they circulate, are based on exchange (178). Once again, representation is crucial for knowledge in the Classical age: "The whole Classical system of order, the whole of that great *taxonomia* that makes it possible to know things by means of the system of their identities, is unfolded within the space that is opened up inside representation when representation represents itself, that area where being and the Same reside" (209). Just as *Don Quixote* occupied a key position on the threshold between the Renaissance and Classicism, so the novels of Sade (*Justine* and *Juliette*), in their representation of the desires of the libertine, are at the threshold of Modern culture (210).

The chapter that opens Part 2 of *The Order of Things* – chapter 7 on "The Limits of Representation" – not only deals with the advent of modernity but also serves to gather together some of the basic procedures and assumptions of the book as a whole. Indeed, the question that sets the direction for Foucault's entire project would seem to be this: "How is it that thought detaches itself from the squares it inhabited before . . . and allows what . . . before had been posited and affirmed in the luminous space of understanding to topple down into error, into the realm of fantasy, into non-knowledge?" (217). In specifying the method of inquiry that will answer this question, Foucault turns directly to the topic announced in his subtitle: *An Archaeology of the Human Sciences*. Such an archaeology, he explains, examines each event it considers in terms of its evident arrangement, the changes in its configuration, and the alterations in the empirical entities that inhabit such positivities as discourse and wealth in the Classical age, which were displaced by language and production during the nineteenth century; furthermore, it will reveal the discontinuities in the organic structures of knowledge as well. Archaeology, then, is a way of doing history that was put into practice during the nineteenth century and continues in full force in *The Order of Things*. It is as though for the first time in human thought (and in Foucault's account of it) the method of interrogating knowledge begins to be examined itself as a mode of knowledge, and history as a succession of events or empiricities is distinguished from History as the arrangement and distribution of empiricities in the space of knowledge. History, for Foucault, is, therefore, "the most erudite, the most aware, the most conscious, and possibly the most cluttered area of our memory; but it is equally the depths from which all beings emerge into their precarious, glittering existence" (219). In the nineteenth century, philosophy occupied the mediating place between history and History, and from Hegel to Nietzsche what it means for thought to have a history became a pressing question. It is also a pressing question for Foucault, and it leads him to a statement of his method of investigation in the form of a purposefully mixed metaphor: "In order to find a way back to the point where the visible forms of beings are joined – the structure of living beings, the value of wealth, the syntax of words

– we must direct our search towards that peak, that necessary but always inaccessible point which drives down, beyond our gaze, towards the very heart of things" (239) ["Pour rejoindre le point où se nouent les formes visibles des êtres – la structure des vivants, la valeur des richesses, la syntaxe des mots – il faut se diriger vers ce sommet, vers cette pointe nécessaire mais jamais accessible qui s'enfonce, hors de notre regard, vers le cœur même des choses" (MC, 252).] To plumb the depths of the very heart of things has been Foucault's ambition throughout this book. For this to be possible, the limits of representation had to be reached, and its hold on the possibilities of knowledge had to be released. This begins to happen in the work of Adam Smith (who recognizes that it is labor not objects whose exchange produces wealth); of Jussieu, Vicq d'Azyr, and Lamarck (whose study of the organic structure of beings begins to focus on the "character" of individuals and species in relation to their functions); and of the first philologists (who shifted the center of gravity of language study from representational naming to the inflectional system and other internal structures of grammar [235]). Simultaneously with these epistemic changes, ideology and critical philosophy begin to separate as a consequence of the work of Destutt de Tracy and Kant. Ideology marked the limit of representation by its situating of all knowledge in the space of representation (240–1).[15]

As Foucault becomes increasingly concerned in Part 2 with the fate of the epistemes in the Modern age, he is simultaneously concerned with closing the gap between history and History, between the intellectual events he considers and the story he tells about them. For this reason, he has increasingly more to say about history, philosophy, and literature in relation to economics, biology, and linguistics. The Modern manner of knowing empiricities, which is the subject of chapter 8, is beset by the challenge of having to work outside the formerly secure space of representation, by the obligation to open up for critical examination, through psychoanalysis and ethnography, the field of human subjectivity, and by the necessity of moving beyond material objectivity in the study of life, labor, and language. The onset of the Modern age is discernible in two phases. From 1775 to 1795, under the impact the works of Adam Smith, A. L. de Jussieu, and John Wilkins, the Classical structure of Western knowledge is on the verge of collapse: "European culture is inventing for itself a depth in which what matters is no longer identities, distinctive characters, permanent tables with all their possible paths and routes, but great hidden forces developed on the basis of their primitive and inaccessible nucleus, origin, causality, and history" (251). The second phase, which opens with the turn of the century, is that of the change in the nature and the form of knowledge. "What changed . . . was knowledge itself as an anterior and indivisible mode of being between the knowing subject and the object of knowledge" (252). For example, in the work of Ricardo all value is seen as having its source in labor; thus, value ceases to be a sign and becomes a product (254). In Cuvier's *Leçons d'anatomie comparée*, the sense of the structure of the organ as an independent entity is replaced by a concern for its function in relation to other organs (264). In the work of such philologists as Bopp and Grimm, words ceased to be fixed structural units of language and came to be understood in terms of their evolutionary history. The similarity here to changes in the life sciences is well captured by a sentence in Schlegel's *On the Language and Philosophy of the Indians* (1808): "The structure or comparative grammar of languages furnishes as certain a key of their genealogy as the study of comparative anatomy has done to the loftiest branch of natural science" (280). Later, Grimm argued in *The Origin of Language* (1859) that not only does language have a history but also that, unlike the anatomy of organs, that of language functions *within* history itself (293). Thus, for the first time since the Renaissance, language resumes its powers of exegesis: "The first book of *Das Kapital* is an exegesis of 'value'; all of Nietzsche is an exegesis of a few Greek words; Freud, the exegesis of all those unspoken phrases that support and at the same time undermine our apparent discourse, our fantasies, our dreams, our bodies" (298). In the Modern age, literature separates itself off from the discourse of ideas, and as a pure manifestation of language becomes obsessed with affirming its own "precipitous" existence (300).

Although the appearance of literature, the return of exegesis, and the development of philology would appear to have eclipsed the concerns of the Classical age, they have not totally displaced them. Indeed, chapter 9 ("Man and His Doubles") envisions Classical knowledge in the Modern age as being in the shade rather than in darkness; it still gives off a blurred light. ["A cette date, il entre, pour tout regard ultérieur, dans une région d'ombre. Encore, n'est-ce pas d'obscurité qu'il faudrait parler, mais d'une lumière un peu brouillée, faussement évidente et qui cache plus qu'elle ne manifeste" (MC, 314).] Foucault is even more explicit about the persistence of the Classical in his essay "What Is Enlightenment?" where he does not hesitate to claim that Kant's reflections on the Enlightenment identified a way of philosophizing that continues to be effective after two centuries:

> The critical ontology of ourselves has to be considered not, certainly, as a theory, a doctrine, not even a permanent body of knowledge that is accumulating; it has to be considered as an attitude, an ethos, a philosophical life in which the critique of what we are is at one and the same time the historical analysis of the limits that are imposed on us and an experiment with the possibility of going beyond them.[16]

"Man" as word and concept is one such limit that has been imposed on the philosophical life and that waits to be breached. "Man," for Foucault, is "a strange empirico-transcendental doublet" in that man in the Modern age – which is to say, in the Classical tradition of the Enlightenment – is both that being in whom knowledge is attained and the one who makes knowledge possible (318). The movement toward this realization can be seen in the return of language to the field of thought, a movement that is an implicit challenge to the reification of literature. Two symptoms of this return are Nietzsche's connections of philosophy with philology and Mallarmé's experiments in enclosing all of discourse within the materiality of the word (305). Like Derrida, Foucault sees the modernist critique of the Classical age as necessarily taking place with the critical methods fashioned by the Enlightenment. But he also sees as the great Modern challenge to both Descartes and Kant the determination to think the unthought, to embrace the obscure Other that is within man (326) ["l'Autre fraternel et jumeau, né non pas de lui, ni en lui, mais à côté et en même temps, dans une identique nouveauté, dans une dualité sans recours" (MC, 337)].

The coming into being of the human sciences, which is the subject of the final chapter of *The Order of Things*, is the predictable outcome of the observation of the Other within man; but as an appropriation of man by the Modern episteme, it also begins the process of man's passing. By becoming the basis on which knowledge is constituted, "man" became the justification for calling into question all knowledge of man (345).[17] Foucault consistently avoids the temptation to assign a privileged position to any of the epistemes or to any of the human sciences, although critique as a procedure fundamental to rational thought, which is the lasting legacy of the Classical age, is for him un-transcendable. As though to emphasize the fact that the human sciences are always subject to their own critical processes, Foucault concludes with an interrogation of psychoanalysis and ethnology, which at the time of the publication of *The Order of Things* had achieved extensive authority and noto-riety as a result of the work of Lacan and Lévi-Strauss. If any modes of knowledge about man would seem to have a commanding presence in the human sciences, they would seem to be psychoanalysis and ethnology. Indeed, none of the other human sciences seems ever to be sure that it is entirely "out of their debt" (379). But despite their pervasive influence, psychoanalysis and ethnology have failed either to arrive at a general concept of man or to be able to do without such a concept. Without ever quite succeeding in establishing a common field, "they ceaselessly 'unmake' that very man who is creating and re-creating his positivity in the human sciences" (379). Although linguistics has been no more successful than psychoanalysis and ethnology in arriving at a general concept of man, the theory of language has become the formal model for psychoanalysis and ethnology (381).

Midway through his book (201), Foucault proposes two diagrams or general tables in an effort to encapsulate his arguments. Unfortunately, however, those diagrams have proved to be notoriously unhelpful.[18] In his excellent book on Foucault, Deleuze offers his own diagram of Foucault's supreme fiction, which looks a bit like a child's drawing of a butterfly. The body is the depth or fold inside knowledge; the upper outline of the outstretched wings is the "line of the outside", the upper pattern on the wings is the strategic zone; and the lower pattern signifies the strata. Deleuze explains that the two wings (as I am calling them) are the two irreducible forms of knowledge, light and language, which capture the thinker in a double movement. On the one hand, we excavate stratum after stratum, following the fissure (or fold) in order to reach the interior of the world of knowledge. But on the other hand and at the same time, we try to climb into a region above the strata in order to understand how light and language relate to each other. The goal of the two movements together is to become both integrated and different, clearly coherent and specifically discrete. Finally, Deleuze claims, we come to realize that the chamber of the fold or fissure is not empty, since one fills it with oneself.[19] As elegant and compelling as Deleuze's summary is, if Foucault's text in some sense is intended to effect a transference with the reader, it may be necessary that no one else's diagram or commentary is ever adequate.

NOTES

1   "Archaeology, Genealogy, Ethics," in *Foucault: A Critical Reader*, ed. David Couzens Hoy (Oxford: Blackwell, 1986), pp. 221–33. The quotation is from "On the Genealogy of Ethics: An Overview of Work in Progress," in *Foucault Reader*, ed. Paul Rabinow (New York: Pantheon, 1984), p. 352.

2   Sheridan's name is for some reason missing from the title page, and he acknowledges his own work only with his initials in the bibliography of his *Foucault: The Will to Truth* (London: Routledge, 1980), p. 227. For Sheridan's comments on the title, see p. 47. The English edition includes a publisher's note (p. viii) on the title. All parenthetical citations are to *The Order of Things: An Archaeology of the Human Sciences* [trans. Alan Sheridan] (New York: Pantheon, 1970).

3   David Macey, *The Lives of Michel Foucault* (London: Hutchinson, 1993), p. 164.

4   *Foucault Live: Interviews 1966–1984*, ed. Sylvère Lotringer (New York: Semiotext(e), 1976), p. 76.

5   On Foucault's militancy, see Macey, *Michel Foucault*, pp. 290–322.

6   There are otherwise, however, profound differences between Foucault's and Habermas's thought, many of which stem from their differing understandings of the Enlightenment and its legacy. See David Ingram, "Foucault and Habermas on the Subject of Reason," in *The Cambridge Companion to Foucault*, ed. Gary Gutting (Cambridge: Cambridge University Press, 1994), pp. 215–61.

7   Roland Barthes, "Taking Sides," in *Critical Essays*, trans. Richard Howard (Evanston, IL: Northwestern University Press, 1972), p. 168.

8   For an excellent account of Freud's poetics and Lacan's response to it, see Malcolm Bowie, *Freud, Proust, and Lacan: Theory as Fiction* (Cambridge: Cambridge University Press, 1987).

9   See Jacques Derrida, *Of Grammatology*, trans. G. C. Spivak (Baltimore: Johns Hopkins University Press, 1976). p. 80; and Edward Said's *Orientalism* (New York: Pantheon, 1978).

10 *Madness and Civilization: A History of Insanity in the Age of Reason*, trans. Richard Howard (New York: New American Library, 1965), p. ix.

11 Ibid.

12 Cf. George Canguilhem's observation that *The Order of Things* is to the sciences of man what *The Critique of Pure Reason* was to the sciences of nature ("The death of man, or exhaustion of the cogito?" trans. Catherine Porter. In *The Cambridge Companion to Foucault*, ed. Gary Gutting [Cambridge: Cambridge University Press, 1994], p. 90.) Canguilhem's review essay is still the best single commentary on *The Order of Things*. See also Gary Gutting, *Michel Foucault's Archaeology of Scientific Reason* (Cambridge: Cambridge University Press, 1989), pp. 139–226. Gutting's judgment of Foucault's book (pp. 225–6), however, unfortunately forgets Foucault's statement of purpose in his preface.

13 Canguilhem, "The death of man," p. 72.

14 See esp. *Of Grammatology*, pp. 14, 158–9.

15 Cf. Althusser on "knowledge of the *ideological field*" in *For Marx*, trans. Ben Brewster (New York: Pantheon, 1969), p. 70.

16 "What Is Enlightenment?," in *The Foucault Reader*; ed. Paul Rabinow (New York: Pantheon, 1984), p. 50.

17 Although he does not exploit this opportunity himself, Foucault here provides a strategic opening for a feminist critique of the concept of man. Cf. Kelly Oliver, *Womanizing Nietzsche: Philosophy's Relation to the "Feminine"* (London: Routledge, 1995), which does not mention Foucault. Lois McNay's excellent *Foucault and Feminism* (Cambridge: Polity Press, 1992) deals with Foucault's later works, especially *The Use of Pleasure* and *The Care of the Self*. See also David M. Halperin, *Saint-Foucault: Towards a Gay Hagiography* (New York: Oxford University Press, 1995), which explores the influence of Foucault's *The History of Sexuality*, volume I on lesbian and gay militants. Halperin's political assessment of James Miller's *The Passion of Michel Foucault* (pp. 143–85) is as important as it is extraordinary.

18 For a commentary on the diagrams, see Pamela Major-Poetzl, *Michel Foucault's Archaeology of Western Culture* (Chapel Hill: University of North Carolina Press, 1983), pp. 156–63.

19 Gilles Deleuze, *Foucault*, trans. Seán Hand (Minneapolis: University of Minnesota Press, 1984), pp. 120–1.

5

Barthes's S/Z

Although Barthes's *S/Z* was published in 1970, just four years after his "Introduction to the Structural Analysis of Narratives," the arguments of the two texts are largely inverted images of each other.[1] The earlier introduction to narratology, which set out to base the study of narrative firmly on linguistics, was also a manifesto for structuralism:

> It is normal that the newly developing structuralism should make [narrative] form one of its first concerns – is not structuralism's constant aim to master the infinity of utterances [*paroles*] by describing the "language" [*"langue"*] of which they are the products and from which they can be generated. Faced with the infinity of narratives, the multiplicity of standpoints – historical, psychological, sociological, ethnological, aesthetic, etc. – from which they can be studied, the analyst finds himself in more or less the same situation as Saussure confronted by the heterogeneity of language [*langage*] and seeking to extract a principle of classification and a central focus for description from the apparent confusion of the individual massages.[2]

S/Z, however, opens by rejecting the practice of Buddhists who attempted to see the whole landscape encapsulated in a single bean. The cost of early narratological studies, including Barthes's, which attempted to see all narratives in a single structure, was great. What got sacrificed in the quest for monomythic unity was the inherent "difference" of each text. The analyst of narrative, then, is faced with the necessity of making an initial methodological choice: "either to place all texts in a demonstrative oscillation, equalizing them under the scrutiny of an 'in-different' science ["la science in-differente" (*S/Z*, 9)], forcing them to rejoin, inductively, the Copy from which we will make them derive; or else to restore each text, not to its individuality, but to its function, making it cohere, even before we talk about it, by the infinite paradigm of difference, subjecting it from the outset to a basic typology, to an evaluation" (3). Whereas in the "Introduction" Barthes chose the first path, in *S/Z* he chooses the second. In two magnificent studies of biblical narrative, his analysis of Genesis 32: 22–32 and Acts 10–11, Barthes makes this change in direction explicit.[3] Judging by his dedication page to *S/Z*, however, the circumstance that led to such a change was his two-year seminar in 1968–9 at the École Pratique des Hautes Études, which was devoted to the study of Balzac's *Sarrasine*. Barthes divides (or pulverizes) that short novella into 561 reading units or lexias, which he groups together under five codes and 48 sequential actions (or "proairetisms"). Barthes then divides his own text into 93 numbered "divagations" (as Richard Howard calls them in his introductory note [x])

In his determination to establish a basic typology of texts, Barthes is setting the direction of his work in part as a response to Foucault's studies of epistemes and Althusser's work on science and ideology. In Barthes's judgment the primary evaluation of a text can be based on neither science nor ideology. Instead, it must be based on the practice of writing. There are, then, two kinds of texts for purposes of primary evaluation: the *writerly* text, which makes the reader a producer of more writing; and the *readerly* text, which makes the reader idle, "intransitive," and serious (4). Barthes's advocacy of the writerly text parallels Foucault's depiction of the Classic literary artifact in contrast to the Modern text, in which thought re-enters literature and productively disrupts it. Here Barthes allies himself with what he calls a "Nietzschean" sense of interpretation (5). In *Beyond Good and Evil* and elsewhere in his writing, Nietzsche employs the metaphor of the world as a text.[4] Such a metaphor has often been read as a categorical rejection of truth and as a characterization of interpretation as the projection of meaning onto a text. But to see a text giving rise to multiple but partial interpretations is not to see its meaning as indeterminate. Rather, it leaves open the possibility of better and more complete readings, each of which may be carried out with complete conviction. What Nietzsche and Barthes opposed was the mistaken view that *only* the methods and objects of science at a particular moment in its history are true. Thus, Nietzsche writes in *The Gay Science*: "That the only justifiable interpretation of the world should be one in which *you* are justified because one can continue to work and do research scientifically in *your* sense (you mean mechanistically?) an interpretation that permits counting, calculating, weighing, seeing, and touching, and nothing more – that is a crudity and naiveté, assuming that it is not a mental illness, an idiocy."[5] Like Foucault, Barthes welcomes a break from the restraints of representation and imitation (5). But in doing so and in celebrating the plurality of the text, he is not carelessly and "in-differently" accepting all interpretations as true (6). The text is reducible neither to what is exterior to it nor to its presumed totality; therefore its narrative structure is never more than a portion of its plurality.

For Barthes, one of the most important developments in linguistics that led to a recognition of textual plurality was Hjelmslev's distinction between denotation and connotation. Because he was convinced that linguistics, like any other science, was responsible in large measure for constructing the objects of its own investigations, Hjelmslev strongly encouraged linguists to reflect on the epistemological consequences of their work.[6] Although Hjelmslev's theory of connotation came to be heavily criticized by semiologists for implying a hierarchy of meaning – "denotation is not the first meaning, but pretends to be so" (9) – Barthes is eager to retain its importance nonetheless, as a basic contribution to understanding textual plurality (8). Because the text is polysemous, reading is far more active and complex a process than the declarative sentence "I read the text" implies. That sequence of subject, verb, object suggests a stable subject acting definitively on a given object, when actually the "I" is a multiplicity already composed of (and by) a plurality of texts before it begins to read the next one. Even the concepts of distinguishable subjectivity and objectivity are reductive images employed to stabilize and to distinguish what is highly mercurial in human experience. Furthermore, reading is not parasitical in relation to a separate, creative, anterior act of writing. Reading is also work, labor, even a species of writing. Here Barthes is highly responsive to Althusser's account of Marx's reading processes;[7] but in order to respond to Althusser and to put forword his own theory of reading, Barthes constructs an extraordinary sentence that wants to capture syntactically the experience of responding to the intertextual plurivocity of texts (10–11): As a form of work, reading is a "lexeological" act that is intimately a part of the production of the text. But just as Marx envisioned a kind of unalienated labor in which the worker was fulfilled in and by labor (e.g. SW, 47), so Barthes sees lexeology as a kind of unalienated reading that is productive of the reader. In this perspective reading ends neither with the text nor with the "I." The proof of such reading lies instead in its function.

> C'est un travail (ce pourquoi il vaudrait mieux parler d'un acte léxéologique – léxéographique, même, puisque j'écris ma lecture), et la méthode de ce travail est topologique: je ne suis pas caché dans le texte, j'y suis seulement irréparable: ma tâche est de mouvoir, de translater des systèmes dont le prospect ne s'arrête ni au texte ni à 《moi》: opératoirement, les sens que je trouve sont avérés, non par 《moi》 ou d'autres mais par leur marque *systématique*: il n'y a pas d'autre *preuve* d'une lecture que la qualité et l'endurance de sa systématique; autrement dit: que son fonctionnement. (S/Z 17)

But the determinable agency here is language itself: "To read, in fact, is a labor of language" (11). As the text, in a sense, passes through me, I work to name, rename, or unname its meanings in a necessarily metonymic labor that forgets even as it struggles to remember. In its inevitable selectivity of attention, reading is made possible by forgetting.

To study texts understood by such a process of reading requires methodological innovation such as that with which Barthes experiments in his reading of *Sarrasine*. Rather than constructing a unified image of the text, as in classic literary study, Barthes's method is an effort to replay the text in slow motion. Reading for him is "decomposition" in the cinematographic sense (12); it is a means of examining a text frame by frame. In such a procedure commentary appears (or interrupts) as digression, which is not traditionally well suited to the discourses of knowledge (13). Although a limited amount of reversibility is possible by replaying portions of the text, such a procedure as Barthes employs adheres to the sequential order of the text, observing thereby its patterns of expectation, repetition, and digression. Because they are determined by their reception, Barthes calls these elemental reading units "lexias." In what appears to be an elaboration of Foucault's image of the trihedron, which for him is a metaphor for the modern episteme[8] – Barthes thinks of the text that is fashioned out of multiple lexias as a polyhedron (14). Presumably any given kind of literary criticism might give priority to one or another side of the text, while Barthes's procedure on the contrary is content to sketch the text's "stereographic" character (15). Furthermore, Barthes's lexeology assumes the necessity of and the desire for multiple readings, rather than a single act of textual consumption.

By simply examining the title and the first sentence of *Sarrasine*, Barthes uncovers the five codes under which all of the story's other textual signifiers can be grouped. Since his method is inductive, the last thing Barthes is proposing is that these five codes are the universal codes of all narratives. Indeed, his advocacy of rereading (16) indicates that they are nothing more permanent than a discernible order arrived at through a particular reading of a given text. Apparently for this reason Barthes has made his exposition of the codes highly dependent on his analysis of the first three lexias in the story. When the reader begins to ask of the title, who or what is Sarassine? the *hermeneutic code* is in operation. It consists of all those units of the text that relate to such a question or constitute such an enigma. As it turns out in this story of sexual ambiguity, the feminine ending (e) is an important signifier in this code. But because femininity in its various connotations combines and interacts with other elements throughout the text, the connotations of femininity comprise the story's *semic code*, which is largely characterized by an instability and dispersion of signification (19). It consists, then, of the connotative signifiers in the lexia (17). The first sentence in

Balzac's story – "I was deep in one of those daydreams" (221) – introduces the vast *symbolic code* of the story, which is rhetorically structured according to familiar patterns of antitheses, such as sleeping and waking, inside and outside, cold and heat, life and death. The main task of this code is to indicate that its multivalent and reversible structure can be entered from almost any point, presumably as soon as its pattern is recognized by the reader (19). For Barthes the word "daydream," for example, reveals the "adversitive" relationship between the key terms that constitute the story's symbolic code. When the reverie of the narrative's first paragraph is interrupted by conversation (lexia #14), the *proairetic code* is introduced. The Aristotelian concept of proairesis refers to the rational ability to determine the result, consequence, or outcome of an action (18). Barthes points out (possibly in opposition to E. M. Forster's famous definition of plot as characters in action) that it is discourse rather than the characters who determine the action in this sense (18). That is because the proairetic code is the result of the reader's amassing and sorting details of events in the story. When a genre of details is given a name, such as "rendezvous" or "murder," the sequence comes into being. Ultimately all of the codes are part of the *cultural code*, which encompasses the various systems of knowledge to which the text refers (18); but strictly speaking the cultural code is introduced in a "collective and anonymous voice originating in traditional human experience" (18). This "gnomic" aspect of the cultural code appears in the subtle means by which the wealth of the Lanty family is established: "the tumultous parties" (lexia #3) and the various details of their life in a private house in the Faubourg Saint-Honoré. Such elements in the cultural code are but references to "a science or body of knowledge," rather than an attempt to reconstruct the culture to which they refer (20).

Barthes is careful in cautioning his reader about the misuse of the codes. He has not attempted to define them more precisely in order to maintain their multivalence and their potential reversibility. Far from being unitary and finite, the text is constantly in motion; and each code is known only by its "departures and returns" (20). The codes are thus "so many fragments of something that has always been *already* read, seen, done, experienced; the code is the wake of that *already*" (20). Each code is not definitively separate from the others, nor is it simply constructed analytically by the reader. The codes are like "off-stage" voices whose origin is lost when they are turned into writing. (Here Barthes is very close to the argument of Derrida's *Of Grammatology*.)[9] The stereographic space of writing is where the codes intersect and where they can be heard as the Voice of Truth (the hermeneutic code), the Voice of the Person (the semic code), the Voice of Symbol (the symbolic code), the

Voice of Empirics (the proairetic code), and the Voice of Science (the cultural code.)

Barthes's concept of science here is remarkably similar to Marx and Engels's, which credits Darwin with a comprehensive understanding of the dialectical processes of nature, in opposition to the monolithic thought of metaphysics. Thus, Engels in *Socialism: Utopian and Scientific* offers this sense of the new (Darwinian) scientific vision: "Every organic being is every moment the same and not the same; every moment it assimilates matter supplied from without, and gets rid of other matter; every moment some cells of its body die and others build themselves anew; in a longer or shorter time the matter of its body is completely renewed, and is replaced by other molecules of matter, so that every organic being is always itself, and yet something other than itself" (SW, 390), The rhetorical equivalent of this scientific vision is antithesis, which is one of the "several hundred figures propounded . . . through the centuries [to] constitute a labor of classification intended to name, to lay the foundations for, the world" (26). Here Barthes cautiously affirms the ambition of the art of rhetoric and, by later extension, the sciences of linguistics, semiotics, and narratology to formulate knowledge of the world. Antithesis consecrates the irreducible division between opposites and, as such, is the most sustained means of affirming difference. (In the first paragraph of *S/Z* Barthes declared that it is difference that "is articulated upon the infinity of texts of languages, of systems" [3].) After a meticulous and systematic analysis of 205 lexias of *Sarrasine*, he arrives at an explanation of the title of his book in terms of his theory of antithesis. Z is the graphological antithesis of S. Furthermore, in the story "Sarrasine contemplates in La Zambinella his own castration" (107). In Barthes's title, then, the slash mark tht separates/joins the S and/from the Z is "the verge of antithesis, the abstraction of limit, the obliquity of the signifier, the index of the paradigm, hence of meaning" (107).[10] It appears, then, that Barthes's selection of this story was not as random as he implies (16).

The climax of the theoretical portion of *S/Z*, like that of Barthes's essay "From Work to Text," is an extended musical metaphor. The lexias are like a succession of measures in an orchestral score, and the codes are like the various instrumental groupings or voices in the composition. Like the brass and percussion parts, the semic, symbolic, and cultural codes stand out in their discontinuity and heavy timbre. The hermeneutic code, like the woodwind melody, unfolds through a series of disclosures and their delayed resolutions, in the manner of a fugue. The proairetic code, like the strings, holds the piece together in a series of actions, familiar cadences, and gestures. The revelation of truth and the coordination of actions are the reading eye's equivalent of tonality. Not only do they limit the plurality of the Classic text; they also, according to Barthes, define the space where the Modern text comes into being (30).

NOTES

1 The British edition mistakenly gives the original date of publication as 1973. Page numbers in parentheses refer to *S/Z*, trans. Richard Miller (Oxford: Blackwell, 1990).

2 "Introduction to the Structural Analysis of Narratives," in *Image – Music – Text*, trans. Stephen Heath (London: Fontana, 1977), p. 80.

3 "The Struggle with the Angel," in *Image – Music – Text*, pp. 125–41, and "L'analyse structurale du récit: à propos d'*Actes* 10–11," in *Exégèse et Herméneutique* (Paris, 1971), pp. 181–204.

4 See, for example, *Beyond Good and Evil*, trans. Walter Kaufmann (New York: Vintage, 1966), pp. 22, 230. One of the best discussions of this metaphor in Nietzsche is Alexander Nehamas, *Nietzsche: Life as Literature* (Cambridge, MA: Harvard University Press, 1985), esp. pp. 62–5.

5 *The Gay Science*, trans. Walter Kaufmann (New York: Vintage, 1974), p. 373.

6 See, for example, Louis Hjelmslev, *Prolegomena to a Theory of Language*, trans. Francis J. Whitfield (Baltimore: Waverly Press, 1953), p. 8.

7 *Reading Capital*, trans. Ben Brewster (London: Verso, 1970), pp. 18–19.

8 *The Order of Things*, trans. Alan Sheridan (New York: Pantheon, 1970), p. 347.

9 Trans. G. C. Spivak (Baltimore: Johns Hopkins University Press, 1976), p. 14.

10 Cf. Lacan's argument that the phallus "is the signifier intended to designate as a whole the effects of the signified, in that the signifier conditions them by its presence as a signifier." He proceeds to claim that the only presence of the phallus in this sense is a dismembered absence – deferred, concealed, and buried ("The Signification of the Phallus," in *Ecrits: A Selection*, trans. Alan Sheridan (London: Tavistock, 1977), p. 285.

6

Althusser's Reading Capital

Even as a material object, the text of *Capital* is extraordinarily complex. Its three intimidating volumes run to approximately 3000 printed pages. Only volume I was published during Marx's lifetime, and his prefaces to the first and second editions of that volume are usually reprinted along with Engels's prefaces to the first English translation and to the fourth German edition. Marx worked on the various portions of his text from 1863 until the end of his life in 1883. Volume III was largely written from 1863 to 1865, before the final draft of volume I was completed, which was in April 1867. Portions of volume II were written before and after the completion of volume I. In his prefaces to volumes II and III, Engels explains the complexities of Marx's manuscripts and describes the difficulties he encountered in editing them for publication, which occurred respectively in 1885 and 1894. It is reasonably certain that considerable portions of volumes II and III were actually written by Engels during this editing process. Marx had planned a fourth volume to contain another massive manuscript that was eventually published in 1905 as a separate work, also in three volumes, under the title *Theories of Surplus Value*. Before his death in 1885, Engels had appointed Karl Kautsky, the editor of *Die Neue Zeit*, to succeed him and to prepare this work for publication. Marx supervised the preparation of a French edition of volume I, which was translated by Joseph Roy and published by Maurice La Châtre in 1872. This edition is discussed by Marx in a letter to La Châtre, which is reprinted in *Reading Capital*.[1] The French text modifed the German edition of 1867 by incorporating Marx's later corrections and additions and, as Marx explains in his letter, by simplifying the text so that it could more easily be read by French workers. Making his text as accessible as possible to the working class was a major concern for Marx. Roy's French translation is the principal text that Althusser deals with in *Reading Capital*, although he refers to the German edition published by Dietz Verlag as well.

Reading Capital is a collection of papers that were written for a seminar on *Capital* at the École Normale Supérieure in 1965. The first edition, which was published the same year, included contributions by Rancière, Macherey, and Establet, which were deleted from the Italian and subsequent English editions in the interest of producing a more manageable book in a single volume. The English edition includes texts by both Althusser and Balibar that are substantially the same as in the first French edition; athough, as Althusser points out in his foreword, the terminology they used had been misread as an implementation of a structuralist ideology. Like Barthes and Foucault, Althusser's understanding of human subjectivity, language, and culture emphasizes plurality and multiplicity rather than individuality and unity. In this sense, structuralism is analogous for him to the German ideology of philosophical idealism against which Marx's thought may be seen as a decisive break.[2]

Although *Capital*, like the Bible, is more widely discussed than carefully read, there are certain ways in which "we have all read, and all do read *Capital*" (13). For a century or more, Althusser claims, we have been able to read it in the details and disputes of our history; we have not been able to escape its arguments in a host of writers who have read it for us; and then there is the opportunity to read especially volume I for ourselves, even though it has often and easily been mistaken for the whole text in its Modern Library and Everyman editions, as well as in Roy's French translation. What Althusser proposes, however, is to read *Capital* completely and "to the letter": that is, he proposes to read it *philosophically*. Whereas economists and historians have read *Capital* without questioning the specificity of its object and the kind of scientific discourse it is, Althusser set out to pose *Capital* "the question of the specific difference both of its object and of its discourse" (14). This meant distinguishing the discourse of *Capital* not only from that of classical economics but also from "the philosophical (ideological) discourse" of the young Marx as found in his writing before *The German Ideology*. Althusser reformulates that epistemological question this way:

> Is *Capital* merely one ideological product among others, classical economics given a Hegelian form, the imposition of anthropological categories defined in the philosophical Early Works on the domain of economic reality; the "realization" of the idealist aspirations of the *Jewish Question* and the *1844 Manuscripts*? Is *Capital* merely a continuation or even culmination of classical political economy, from which Marx inherited both object and concepts? And is *Capital* distinguished from classical economics not by its object, but only by its *method*, the dialectic he borrowed from Hegel? Or, on the contrary, does *Capital* constitute a real epistemological mutation of its object, theory and method? Does *Capital* represent the founding moment of a new discipline . . . the absolute beginning of the history of a science? (15)

To ask such a question as this has enormous implications, not only for an understanding of Marx but also for an understanding of philosophy and of critical reading.

Althusser anticipates that when the history of the second half of the twentieth century is one day viewed from a critical distance, it will appear as a time in human culture when the simplest acts of existence – seeing, listening, speaking, reading – were systematically investigated and taught. In this respect the thought and example of Marx, Nietzsche, and Freud provide a lasting epistemological legacy. This does not mean, however, that one can now read Marx simply by imitating the way he read others, because he did not read just one way. Sometimes, as in the *1844 Manuscripts*, Marx simply read "at sight," innocently assuming, according to Althusser, that the essence of the human historical world could transparently be read in its concrete existence. When he read this way, he shared uncritically a religious myth of reading with Galileo, who set out to read the Great Book of the World (16). In his early work, therefore, Marx was still in the grip of what Foucault refers to as the episteme of representation. In *Capital*, however, Marx's reading acknowledges the "opacity of the immediate" (16) and the difference that implies between the imaginary and the true. Althusser credits Spinoza with having initiated reading of this sort. Here Althusser seems to be going beyond Marx and Engels's few scattered references to Spinoza (e.g. SW, 328, 388) to Spinoza's own theory of reading in his *Theologico-Political Treatise*, chapter IX, which is a foundational text for critical theory.[3] In his determination to read the Bible to the letter, Spinoza faced similar problems to those that Lacan would confront when he read Freud and that Althusser here encounters when he sets out to read Marx in the same way. First, there is the accumulation of earlier readings (or misreadings), which Spinoza found in the Bible's marginalia; and second, there is the fact that the Bible (like Freud and Marx) does not say just one thing. To read it with any integrity requires making the critical distinction between meaning and truth, or for Althusser between the imaginary and the true. His term "the imaginary" is derived from Lacan to signify an anticipated wholeness or unity, the absence of which alienates the reader from the text. For Spinoza that distinction is powerfully related to that between a real object and the idea of the object, which is the substance of knowledge. Both distinctions took on a fundamental importance for Marx, according to Althusser (40).

Perhaps the most important consequence of reading *Capital* totally and to the letter is that this procedure allows the text to instruct the reader in how it is to be read. Thus, Althusser candidly admits that what he had thought to be his own critical discoveries, which he reported in *For Marx*, he later found already present in what Marx and Engels had written in *Capital* (28–29n). The details of the text that Althusser had missed, which were in the forms of buried allusion and argument by metaphor, take on considerable importance in *Reading Capital*. In order to clarify the kind of reading he thinks *Capital* requires, Althusser provides a detailed account of Marx's reading of Smith and Ricardo (18–30), which appears in one of the sections of *Capital* that Althusser had previously neglected (CI, 537–8). Sometimes when Marx reads classical economists, his is a "retrospective theoretical reading" (18), in which he assesses Smith's or Ricardo's strengths and weaknesses and then supplements their texts with what they had missed. Although Althusser does not cite this example, in *Value, Price and Profit* Marx points out that Ricardo succeeded in destroying the fallacy that wages determine prices, while Smith is inconsistent on this point, anticipating Ricardo in his more scientific research but employing the fallacy nonetheless in other parts of his writing (SW, 191). Here Marx corrects Smith's inconsistency by invoking Ricardo's *On the Principles of Political Economy*. To supplement the thought of one text with that of a later one is, of course, an ordinary protocol of critical reading. There is, however, a very different sort of reading, which Althusser calls "symptomatic reading" (28). What is at stake here is not simply the completness or consistency of what is seen but rather the manner of seeing itself and how that seeing in turn determines the object of vision. The oversight that is exposed by this means is a non-vision inside vision (21). On this point Engels made an apt comparison between Joseph Priestley's discovery of oxygen by means of phlogistic chemistry and classical economists' discovery of surplus value (CII, 15). The non-vision within both instances of vision provided the means of subsequently revolutionizing all of chemistry and economics. Such moments in the history of a science reveal its enabling limitations: "it can only pose problems on the terrain and within the horizon of a definite theoretical structure, its problematic, which constitutes the absolute and definite condition of possibility, and hence the absolute determination of *the forms in which all problems must be posed*" (25). The achievement of *Capital* was to revolutionize the old problematic of economics – Foucault calls it the episteme of wealth – in its totality.

Having established the distinction between Marx's retrospective theoretical reading and his symptomatic reading, Althusser moves on in Part II of *Reading Capital* to give an account of the object of *Capital* that is the product of Marx's unique method of analysis. Althusser explains (73) that in the division of labor that was part of the arrangements for the 1965 seminar, it fell to him to treat Marx's relation to his work. By searching Marx's texts for his "image" of his undertaking, Althusser is also in search of "the fundamental epistemological

question which constitutes the object of Marxist philosophy itself"(73). Once
Marx identifies the ideological pretensions of German idealism, which were
part of his own early work; once he breaks with that ideology in the determination not just to understand the world but also to change it with the power
of revolutionary knowledge; and once he has laboriously conducted the primary
research necessary to understand the capitalist mode of production, which
ruptures Hegel's teleological hope for "the religious triumph of reason" (44) –
where then does that leave philosophy? In his attempt to answer this question
Althusser first turned to those texts by Marx that seem explicitly to reflect
upon his own philosophical procedure: the *1857 Introduction to a Contribution
to the Critique of Political Economy* and the second chapter of *The Poverty of
Philosophy*. In reading these texts, however, Althusser encounters two problems. First, although they provide the means for recognizing the object of
Marxist philosophy, they do not offer an explicit concept of it. Second, in order
to compare the state of philosophy before and after Marx's epistemological
break with German philosophical ideology, it is necessary to adopt Marx's
method of symptomatic reading and his philosophical principles. In short,
those critical questions one wants most to ask of Marx are precisely those
which, by his own example, he teaches his reader to ask. It now becomes clear
why Althusser earlier (15) calls philosophical reading "guilty reading": once
one encounters Marx's critical philosophical practice (his "symptomatic reading"), all innocence is lost. Or, as another of Althusser's metaphors implies, it
is not possible to compare the portions of philosophy that Marx has illumi-
nated with what was (or is) in the shade (73), because even to begin to make
such a comparison is to cast a Marxist critical light into the shade. The specific
difference of the object of *Capital*, then, "is both visible and hidden, present
and absent . . . for reasons arising from the very *nature* of its presence, from the
disconcerting novelty of Marx's revolutionary discovery" (78). Like all radical
innovations, Marx's discovery is blinding.

As Althusser points out (80), Marx often summed up his discovery as
consisting of three concepts: value and use-value, abstract labor and concrete
labor, and surplus-value. The unique feature of these concepts, Althusser
insists, is that they are designed to overcome abstraction, or the distinction
between the idea of an object and the object itself. Here "scientific abstractions
exist in the state of empirical realities" (124). But even as early as 1895, in an
exchange between Conrad Schmidt and Engels over Marx's concept of value,
this unique feature of Marx's concepts begins to get lost. While Schmidt refers
to Marx's law of value as a necessary "theoretical fiction," Engels provides the
weak defense that all concepts can be regarded as such "from the standpoint of
reality" (82). This is a prime instance of theoretical blindness, which Althusser

believes occurs whenever the question of Marx's unique object of knowledge is neglected.

One useful way of determining the object (or image) of Marx's work is to consider what he took to be the merits and errors of classical economists. For example, in *Theories of Surplus Value* he acknowledges his predecessors who isolated the concepts of value and surplus-value even though they did not completely develop or refine those concepts. But perhaps even more important, he credits Smith and Ricardo with having treated political economy scientifically by reducing phenomena to essences and by dealing with essences systematically. However, his fundamental criticism of classical economics, which runs from *The Poverty of Philosophy* to *Capital*, is that its conception of the economic categories of capitalism is ahistorical. As Althusser understands it, Marx's concept of historical time is based on "the complex and differentially articulate structure that is in dominance within the social totality arising from a determinable mode of production" at a given moment (108). (Here one might speculate, for example, whether the computerization of Western academic life is once again the result of intellectuals becoming the uncritical conduits of capitalist ideology, who perpetuate corporate interests by making students dependent on computer technology to the point at which they cannot carry out basic mathematical and language functions any other way than on a computer.) Because such structures of dominance require critical processes to unmask them, historical time is a "theoretical concept [that] is aimed directly at historians and their practice" (109). Althusser thus concludes that:

> The object of history as a science therefore has the same kind of theoretical existence and occupies the same theoretical level as the object of Marx's political economy. The only difference that can be established between the theory of political economy, of which *Capital* is an example, and the theory of history as a science, lies in the fact that the theory of political economy only considers one relatively autonomous component of the social totality, whereas the theory of history in principle takes the complex totality as such for its object. Other than this difference, there can be no distinction between the science of political economy and the science of history, from a theoretical view-point. (109)

The theory of history, therefore, makes it possible to see and to know the structures of dominance which constitute temporal reality.

Is Marxism, then, a historicism in the sense of its object being both an evolved outcome and an activity of knowledge defined by the present? Althusser insists that it is not. Indeed, he argues that "*theoretically speaking,* Marxism is, in a single movement and by virtue of the unique epistemological rupture which established it, an anti-humanism and an anti-historicism" (119). The origin of this error, which Althusser is determined to correct, lies both in the circumstances of the 1917 Revolution and in the writings of Gramsci, Colletti, and Sartre. Even more important, there is a certain ambiguity or conceptual indistinctness in some of Marx's own writing (for example, in the *1857 Introduction* and in volume I of *Capital* [CI, 75]) that invite such a misreading. However, Marx's usual view is that what saves science from naive and stagnant retrospection, which Hegel had warned against in his *Introduction to the Philosophy of History*, is self-criticism. Without historical self-criticism even such a brilliant thinker as Aristotle failed to understand value and labor because he thought only within the limits of his present (123). Thus, Marx writes, "Aristotle could not read out of the value form of commodities the fact that all labour is here expressed as indistinct human labour, and consequently as labour of equal quality, *because* Greek society was founded upon slave-labour, and had therefore, for its natural basis the inequality of men and of their labour powers" (CI, 59–60). In a systematic survey of classical political economists, Marx observed their inability to "run ahead of their times" (123). The most important epistemological achievement of Smith and Ricardo, however, was that "they attained science itself in the consciousness of their present because this consciousness was, as a consciousness, *its own self-criticism, i.e., a science of itself*" (123). In place of such self-criticism that kept Marx from simply reifying his own present, Gramsci puts the consciousness of the ideology of the ruling hegemonic class, Colletti places the hypothetical or experimental processes of history, and Sartre substitutes human "praxis" or human inter-subjectivity as a whole.

It is constantly necessary in order to be true to Marx's text to be vigilantly critical of it, and it is in this context of his affirmation of Marx's self-criticism that Althusser offers his most eloquent statement of his own procedure in *Reading Capital*:

> In an epistemological and critical reading . . . we cannot but hear behind the proffered word the silence it conceals, see the blank of suspended rigour, scarcely the time of a lightning-flash in the darkness of the text: correlatively, we cannot but hear behind this discourse which seems continuous but is really interrupted and governed by the threatened irruption of a repressive discourse, the silent voice of the real discourse, we cannot but restore its text, in order to re-establish its profound continuity. It is here that the identification of the precise points of weakness in Marx's rigour is the same thing as the recognition of that rigour: it is his rigour that shows us its weaknesses; and in the brief moment of his temporary silence we are simply returning to him the speech that is his own. (143–4)

This brings Althusser back to the question of Marx's object in *Capital*.

After such elaborate preparation, it may at first be disappointing to find Althusser announcing at last that surplus-value as both term and concept is the object of *Capital*. Engels anticipated such a response with his question,

> But what is there new in Marx's utterances on surplus-value? How is it that Marx's theory of surplus-value struck home like a thunderbolt out of a clear sky, and that in all civilized countries . . . the theories of all his socialist predecessors . . . vanished without having produced any effect? (CII, 14)

In answer to this question Althusser points out that because they lacked the term and concept of surplus-value, Smith and Ricardo constantly confused it with its forms of existence as profit, rent, and interest. Marx and Engels, on the other hand, clearly understood that terminological innovation was an important step in the history of science in opening up new conceptual space (CI, 4–6). As Althusser perceptively puts it, the failure of the classical economists to think surplus-value "in a word which was the concept of its object" kept them imprisoned in ideology and in the empirical concepts of economic practice (148). Their position was to Marx's what Priestley's was to Lavoisier's: Priestley produced oxygen without knowing what he had produced, while Lavoisier's production generated for him not a solution but a problem that resulted in the discrediting of the mistaken categories of phlogistic chemistry and the founding of the modern science of chemistry (CII, 14–16). Like Priestley, who refused to give up his phlogistic theory, Smith and Ricardo refused to question the "theoretical problematic" which their own investigations had begun to discredit. But finally, surplus-value is not just one economic fact among others. By providing the basis for understanding all capitalist production, it was destined to revolutionize all of economics (155). Marx defines the concept (or reality) of surplus-value simply as "the difference between the value of the product and the value of the elements consumed in the formation of that product, in other words, of the means of production and the labour-power" (CI, 201).

There are two major consequences for anthropology, Althusser argues, in Marx's revolutionary impact on economics. One is that the uncritical assumption of a homogeneous *Homo oeconomicus* is discredited by Marx's demonstration that needs are not absolute givens of the human condition but are historically determined. Consumption is not for Marx a matter of human nature but the result of disposable income and available products (166). Marx's thought is correspondingly unreceptive to the declaration that labor constitutes the essence of man, which is a common ideological view of existential Marxism.

Once Marx's thought is seen as critically disruptive of a static and unreflective image of human beings, a second consequence follows: The "economic" ceases to be a category or level in society, history, or anthropology. Instead, it becomes the articulation of the relations of production that permeate society but seem to be strategically concealed in modern life (179).

Althusser concludes by arguing that it is a mistake to think of the journey from volume I to volume III of *Capital* as a move from the abstract to the concrete. Marx never leaves knowledge (the "product of thinking and conceiving" [190]) because, given his object, there is no frontier or homogeneous space between the abstract and the empirical, the concept and the concrete. Indeed, his persistent project was to account theoretically for the effect of a structure on its elements. In doing so, he wrestled with the several potentially relevant epistemological categories that were part of his intellectual inheritance: phenomena and essence, the essential and the inessential, the real and the meaningful, the inside and the outside. Although he occasionally lapses into these received categories himself, Marx manages nonetheless to fashion a new conceptual language in *Capital*, "a language of metaphors which are nonetheless, already *almost perfect concepts*, and which are perhaps only incomplete insofar as they have not yet been *grasped*" (192). The considerable achievement of Althusser's own experimental text is to illuminate those metaphors as the places in Marx's writing where truth breaks through in all its power, complexity, and strangeness.

NOTES

1   *Reading Capital*, trans. Ben Brewster (London: Verso, 1970), p. 9. All further references to this text appear in parentheses. For more details concerning the production of the text of *Capital*, see David McLellan, *The Thought of Karl Marx: An Introduction* (New York: Harper and Row, 1971), p. 84, and *Karl Marx: His Life and Thought* (New York: Harper and Row, 1973), pp. 338–53.
2   The most reliable, detailed studies of Althusser's thought are Robert P. Resch, *Althusser and the Renewal of Marxist Social Theory* (Berkeley: University of California Press, 1992) and Gregory Elliott, *Althusser: The Detour of Theory* (London: Verso, 1987).
3   See Christopher Norris, *Spinoza and the Origins of Modern Critical Theory* (Oxford: Blackwell, 1990).

7

Signs, Images, and the Real: Barthes, Althusser, and Foucault on Photography and Painting

A great number of ordinary words and expressions having to do with knowledge or thought are directly or indirectly related to vision. A random sample includes *demonstrate, enlighten, examine, foresee, imagine, insight, inspect, outlook, point of view, prospect, reflect, scope, speculation, survey, synopsis, theory:* also *voir, pouvoir, savoir.*[1] Given the ubiquitousness of visual metaphors in the discourses of knowledge, it is not surprising that Barthes, Althusser, and Foucault included a critical examination not only of the imagery of knowledge and thought in their continuing project of uncovering the foundations of human understanding but also a systematic investigation of the visual arts as well. Barthes was fascinated by photography throughout his professional life, both because of its power to capture the dynamics of human subjectivity and because of its ability to register the semiotics of cultures. Although he makes important use of the medium in his autobiography and in his book on Japan (*The Empire of Signs*), he dealt systematically and at length with the medium only in his last book, *Camera Lucida*, where his attention falls principally on portrait photography. Althusser wrote very little about the visual arts, but what he did write has been largely neglected by his commentators. Actually, he was for a considerable time fascinated by the modern Italian painter Leonardo Cremonini, whose work seemed to be prescient in anticipating the critique of humanist ideology that engaged Althusser in all of his writings. Foucault, of course, had written a major piece on Velázquez as the opening chapter of *The Order of Things*. But Magritte's language paintings seemed uncannily to have anticipated Foucault's genealogical studies of systems of thought. The driving interest in what Barthes, Althusser, and Foucault write about the visual arts is their search for a means of understanding the rival claims of the visual and the verbal – the sign and the image – in laying a foundation for knowledge. All three writers were in search of the ways the real relates to images and to signs.

Barthes's *Camera Lucida*

As he indicates on his dedication page,[2] Barthes wrote *Camera Lucida* in homage to Jean-Paul Sartre's book *L'Imaginaire* (1940), which had been published 40 years earlier and was later translated as *The Psychology of Imagination*. This dedication may be simultaneously genuine and ironic. Barthes's affirmation of Sartre went back at least as far as 1945, to the founding of the journal *Les Temps modernes*, whose manifesto had a profound effect on Bathes when he was being treated for tuberculosis at a student sanatorium in Touvet.[3] In his introduction to the first issue of the new journal Sartre had written, "We situate ourselves on the side of those who want to change both the social condition of Man, and his own self-conception."[4] For Barthes to affirm Sartre's *L'Imaginaire* in 1980, however, could not help but be read, at least in part, as an implicit critique of Lacan, whose famous theory of the mirror stage was nevertheless extremely important for Barthes.

It is particularly Sartre's distinction between the sign and the photographic image (chapter 2, part 2) that Barthes appropriates and quietly modifies in *Camera Lucida*. When one looks at a photograph, Sartre writes, what one sees is the "physical individuality" of the person.[5] Sartre's general project in *The Psychology of Imagination* was to investigate the intentional structure of the image and thus implicitly to challenge Hegel's conception of a unified self with the idea of consciousness as a multiplicity of psychical structures. Thus, the aim of his study of imagination, like the founding purpose of *Les Temps modernes*, was to change the self-conception of human beings, specifically by describing a neglected function of consciousness: the imagination and its noetic correlative, the imaginary. Here Sartre alludes to Husserl, who argues in his celebrated book *Ideas* that intentional consciousness includes noetic elements that bestow order and meaning on sensory materials that are passively received by the mind.[6]

In the course of his description of the imagination, Sartre distinguishes between the sign and the image. There is "no relationship whatsoever," he argues, between the sign *Office*, for example, and that complex physical and social object that it signifies, whereas the photographic image of Peter *resembles* him. Sartre demonstrates that this distinction between sign and image is commonly confused in classical psychology. In a photographic image, according to Sartre, the resemblance is "prior to all interpretation," and it invites the viewer to make a perceptual synthesis that enables the portrait photograph "to stand for Peter in person." Therefore, to say "This is Peter" is to enter into an imagined synthesis.[7] Sartre summarizes his distinction this way:

> As meaning, a word is but a beacon: it presents itself, awakens a meaning, and
> this meaning never returns to the word but goes out to the thing and the word
> is dropped. In the case of the physical image, however, the intentionality
> constantly returns to the image-portrait. We face the portrait and we *observe it*;
> the imaginary consciousness of Peter is being constantly enriched; new details
> are being constantly added to the object: that wrinkle I had not noticed in Peter
> until I saw it in his portrait becomes a regular part of his features from now on.
> Each detail is perceived, but not for itself, not as a spot of color on a canvas: it
> becomes a part of the object at once, that is, a part of Peter.[8]

Peter in person is thus changed, in the eyes of the spectator, by his photograph.
Furthermore, Sartre claims, the image makes present what is absent or dead.
It is only in reflective consciousness, which reveals the function fulfilled by the
photograph, that one thinks of the photograph "as an image of Peter." Unlike
the sign, which does not deliver its object, "the picture . . . *delivers* Peter,
though Peter is not here."[9] During the 40 years after Sartre wrote these words,
everything he had to say about the sign and the image would be subjected to
a sustained critique, especially by Derrida. Four years before Sartre's book
appeared, however, Lacan had already laid the foundation for that critique in
his paper on "The Mirror Stage."[10] Since Lacan's paper was not in fact published until 1949, although it had first been delivered as a conference presen-
tation in 1936, it is not clear whether the eventual published form of the paper
was in part written after and partly in response to Sartre's *L'Imaginaire*.

Lacan observed that when small children become fascinated by their own
reflection in a mirror, they begin to fall into the trap of imagining themselves
as a unified being (or ego) established and functioning in the world. But this
early defining image of the future human subject has a tragically alienating
consequence. While imagining a future of full, stable, and unified identity, the
subject also knows that he or she has not—indeed, cannot – become that image.
Thus the subject lives in a continuous state of longing for an always receding
future, a future that will never arrive. The imaginary, for Lacan, is a stage or
mode of being in which the human subject is in the throes of a desire for ego
integrity, individuality, and identity, while simultaneously beginning to recognize that she or he is perpetually caught between a lost maternal past and an
unreachable illusion of an integrated and individuated future.[11] Lacan later
developed his theory of the mirror stage to include a theory of the gaze, based
in part on Dali's concept of paranoic knowledge. According to this theory,
paintings – and here Holbein's *The Ambassadors* is Lacan's prime example – are
not passively receptive objects of our investigation. Instead, it is they who fix
the viewer with *their* gaze, thereby holding the observer in thrall.[12]

The opening pages of *Camera Lucida* allude extensively to Sartre's and Lacan's rival theories of the imaginary, and one of the many ambitions of Barthes's poignant and beautifully written book is to negotiate between them. He does this by critically appropriating and then supplementing Sartre's and Lacan's texts. In his opening paragraph Barthes sounds some of the major themes of his book. *Camera Lucida* is largely a first-person narrative, which in many ways complements and completes his highly unconventional autobiography, *Roland Barthes par Roland Barthes* (1975). Barthes opens his study of photography with the recollection of looking at a photograph of Napoleon's youngest brother, which in turn triggers another story, that the eyes of the brother in the photograph are those that once looked on Napoleon. But these linked stories are almost immediately forgotten as Barthes's interests in photography become more broadly cultural and as he pursues his "ontological" desire to discover what photography is in itself. This pursuit leads him to oppose photography to cinema, even though he was unable definitively to separate photography from it. His doubt, however, persisted that photography might not have in fact a unique "genius" or mode of being.

Nevertheless, photography seems to evade all distinctions we might wish to impose upon it. What is unique about the semiotics of the photograph – and here Barthes resists Sartre's certainty in distinguishing the image from the sign – is that the photograph "reproduces to infinity what has occurred only once" in that it enables the viewer to look repeatedly at a moment of the real that can never be repeated existentially, because, for example, Napoleon's youngest brother is dead. Insofar as it is a sign – and Barthes is reluctant to say that it is or is not a sign – any specific photograph is indistinguishable from its referent. Unlike Magritte's famous painting of a pipe with the accompanying caption, "This is not a pipe," a pipe in a photograph, Barthes insists, "is always and intractably a pipe" (5). Given its lamination to its object, photography as medium is largely invisible. Thus, Barthes confesses, what is written about photography seems to have nothing to do with photographs or with such referents as a desired object or a beloved body. Photography, then, simultaneously resists being abstracted from its referent(s) or reduced to a single element or principle. The recognition of the uniqueness of photography led Barthes to take himself "as mediator for all Photography" (8) in order to capture the universal particularity of the medium. It is, however, as spectator and observed subject, rather than photographer, that Barthes proposes to make himself "the measure of photographic 'knowledge'" (9).

The problem with being a subject observed by the lens of the camera is that, in posing for the camera, one takes on another body and transforms oneself into an image. It is not just that the photograph creates a new body in the picture; it also "mortifies" (11) the body of the observed subject. Photography is thus an art of absence and death for Barthes. This is, of course, not what one wants from photographs, only what one gets from them. What one wants but does not get (cannot get) is a mobile image of one's profound self, but there is never a coincidence of oneself with the image of oneself. In the photograph the self becomes an other: "a cunning dissociation of consciousness from identity" (12). Thus, to refer to any human subject as *one*-self is always misleading.

The importance of the photographic image for the formation of the self is the continuing theme of *Roland Barthes par Roland Barthes*. Unlike *Camera Lucida*, in which photographic images are interlaced with the verbal text, *Roland Barthes* opens with several pages of visual images to which the verbal text is subordinated. The entire book is an autobiographical elaboration of Freud's theory of the imago and Barthes's subtle assessment of the rival claims of Lacan and Sartre concerning the imaginary. Although Barthes seems to stress the importance of the imaginary, it is actually more the Freudian underpinnings of Lacan's and Sartre's theories that he actually deals with in his account of the development of his own subjectivity. For Freud, the term *imago* refers to the child's internalized image of its parents' authority and affection, which enables the child to retain its past without being bound to it during the process of normal development (SE, XI: 181; XII: 100; XIX: 168). In short, the imago is fundamental to the production of the dynamic self. Although Freud uneasily held out the hope of eventual ego integration (SE, XXII: 80), Barthes assumes, with Lacan, the inescapable division of the human subject, which nevertheless coexists with the subject's longing for integration. Indeed, human subjectivity in this context is division longing for integration. When he looks at photographs – especially those of himself – Barthes insists, "I *see* the fissure in the subject" (*RB*, 3). Although deceptively innocent, a picture of his mother holding the infant Barthes is a powerful illustration of the concept of the imago. The eyes of mother and child look directly into the camera, and the caption reads, "The mirror stage: 'That's you'" (*RB*, 21). Since the point of view of the entire book is that of Barthes writing about himself in the third person, as though he were "a character in a novel" (*RB*, 1), it is as though his mother is speaking from the picture to Barthes as narrator about himself as infant. Thus, here Barthes plays his two photographic roles – observer and observed subject – at once, but in doing so he eloquently displays his divided self. In a later section of this disrupted narrative of his life, which superficially appears to be an arbitrarily arranged series of alphabetical entries, Barthes devotes a comparatively long section to the structure of his text, a section he entitles "The circle of fragments":

To write by fragments: the fragments are then so many stones on the perimeter of a circle: I spread myself around: My whole little universe in crumbs; at the center, what? (*RB*, 92–3)

Like Deleuze, who models his texts on the *assemblage* in order to manifest the multiplicity of the subject, Barthes writes in fragments, breaks up those fragments with alluring visual images, and refers to himself in the third person in order to capture the "profound self" that is caught between fissure and wholeness.

At least part of Barthes's project here is polemical. In an essay entitled "The Great Family of Man," which was later published in his book *Mythologies*, he had reviewed an exhibition of photographs entitled *The Family of Man*, which was launched at the Museum of Modern Art in New York in 1955. In book form the collection of 503 images became one of the best-selling exhibitions of photographs ever published.[13] The implied thesis of the exhibition was that not only are individual human beings unified but so is the whole family of man. Defying all forms of cultural difference, *The Family of Man* juxtaposes images of human beings in love or in despair in order to promote the idea of a universal and culturally transcendent humanity. The ideology of the exhibition is set forth in Carl Sandberg's prologue:

The first cry of a newborn baby in Chicago or Zamboango, in Amsterdam or Rangoon, has the same pitch and key, each saying, "I am! I have come through! I belong! I am a member of the Family."[14]

André Chamson's introductory leaflet for the showing in Paris, on the other hand, was appropriately skeptical: "This look over the human condition must somewhat resemble the benevolent gaze of God on our absurd and sublime ant-hill."[15] Barthes's basic objection to the exhibition was its mystification of the human condition, "which always consists in placing Nature at the bottom of History."[16] Thus, for a classical humanist there is an irreducible human nature that lies beneath the historical diversities of human culture.

But without history, Barthes observes, there is nothing to be said about such facts of nature as birth and death. At the time he reviewed *The Family of Man* in 1955, Barthes believed that both the exhibition and photography as a medium failed to be historically significant:

The failure of photography seems to be flagrant in this connection: to reproduce death or birth tells us, literally, nothing. For these natural facts to gain access to a true language, they must be inserted into a category of knowledge which means postulating that one can transform them, and precisely subject their naturalness to our human criticism.[17]

By the time he wrote *Camera Lucida*, Barthes's assessment of photography had radically changed. Whereas he had been heavily under the influence of his first reading of Saussure's *Course in General Linguistics* when he reviewed *The Family of Man*, his later meditations on photography were less bound by the Saussurean separation of the sign from what it signifies. The major change in Barthes's thinking appears in his 1961 essay, provocatively entitled, "The Photographic Message." There he argues that the photographic image has the power to transmit literal reality. Even though it reduces what it transmits, the photograph does not transform it. While it is not to be confused with reality itself, it is nevertheless the "analogical perfection" of the real. Indeed, "it is a message without a code."[18] As such, it qualifies as a category of knowledge.

In 1977 Barthes's mother died. Two years before, he had published *Roland Barthes*; and three years later, the year of his own death, he was to publish *Camera Lucida*. Whereas *Roland Barthes* is written in the third person, *Camera Lucida* is an insistently first-person text. Indeed, some of the most insistently first-person narrations – such as Thoreau's *Walden* and Dostoevsky's *Notes from Underground* – are studies in divided selves and alienated subjectivity. Barthes partly explains the urgency of this book as a matter of commitment to exploring himself as a spectator. The "I" who is the subject of no less than twelve sentences in the book's short opening paragraph is to be seen not as a question of theme "but as a wound: I see, I feel, hence I notice, I observe, and I think" (21). For Barthes the experience of being the spectator of a photograph is one in which he is neither subject nor object; rather, he is "a subject who feels he is becoming an object." As he views the photograph, he becomes a "specter" and experiences "a micro–version of death" (14). Furthermore, when he looks at a photograph of himself, he discovers that he has become "Total-Image, which is to say, Death in person" (14). Now that Barthes is in fact dead, looking at such photographs of him as those he includes in *Roland Barthes* (RB, 24, 25, 28, 37) with the awareness that he is no longer alive gives an added significance to his announcement that "Ultimately, what I am seeking in the photograph taken of me (the "intention" according to which I took at it) is Death: Death is the *eidos* of the Photograph" (15). Here Barthes boldly names the intentional structure of the image, which Sartre wanted to divorce from the sign. Death is the referent, signification, or *eidos* of the photograph in several senses: The body while posing becomes distorted and mortified before the lens. While still living, the subject catches a glimpse of a lost moment in his life when he looks at a photograph of himself. But such images also capture the illusory hope of an integrated future for the subject.

Because Barthes's mother was such a defining presence in his life and in the photographs taken of them together (*RB*, 5, 20, 21, 27) and because she provided him with a "family without familialism" (*RB*, 27), her death seems to have precipitated the death of Barthes himself. Barthes nursed her throughout her final illness, during which she seemed to him to become his little girl (72): or, more precisely, she became united for him with the image of herself as a child, which he refers to as the Winter Garden Photograph. He cannot, he insists, reproduce that photograph because it exists only for him and because it would not wound any other spectator as it does him. Nevertheless, there in that elusive image floated the essence of the photograph; and there too was the Ariadne's thread that would lead him to understand his fascination with photography.

The story Barthes tells about that photograph is extraordinarily moving. After his mother's death he went to the apartment where she died to sort though her things. He found her collection of photographs and began to look through them, searching "for the truth of the face I had loved" (67). Then, suddenly, he discovered the sepia Winter Garden print of his mother at age 5. As he looks at the face of the little girl, Barthes eventually discovers the face of his mother; or rather the essence of her innocence and gentleness are apparent to him in her little girl's countenance. Like Proust's photograph of his grandmother or Nadar's of his mother, the Winter Garden Photograph of Barthes's mother was a "supererogatory" image that "contained more than what the technical being of photography can reasonably offer" (70): It achieved for him "the impossible science of the unique being" (71).

Although Barthes explicitly denies that there is a center to be found in the midst of his labyrinthine narrative (73), a key passage in his book is the one that joins his mother's death to an uncanny anticipation of his own:

> At the end of her life, shortly before the moment when I looked through her pictures and discovered the Winter Garden Photograph, my mother was weak, very weak. I lived in her weakness (it was impossible for me to participate in a world of strength, to go out in the evenings; all social life appalled me). During her illness, I nursed her, held the bowl of tea she liked because it was easier to drink from than from a cup; she had become my little girl, uniting for me with that essential child she was in her first photograph . . . Ultimately I experienced her, strong as she had been, my inner law, as my feminine child. Which was my way of resolving Death . . . I who had not procreated, I had, in her very illness, engendered my mother. Once she was dead I no longer had any reason to attune myself to the progress of the superior Life Force (the race, the

species). My particularity could never again universalize itself (unless, utopically, by writing, whose project henceforth would become the unique goal of my life). From now on I could do no more than await my total, undialectical death. (71–2)

Here the Winter Garden Photograph, which he was not to find until after his mother had died, enables Barthes to understand how his mother, in her dying weakness, had become his child, or rather the "essential child." For him the essence of his mother – her innocent gentleness – was suspended between her dying weakness and her 5-year-old image. But as he looks at that image of the person who was the source of his own imago, he realizes that the photograph's referent is not just lost maternal innocence, his mother's death, or even death itself. What the photograph finally captures is his own "undialectical death." Such is the wound or ultimate referent of this photograph and of all photography.

However much he reworks the theoretical ground that Sartre staked out in *L'Imaginaire*, Barthes's own distinctive theoretical vocabulary slowly surfaces in Part 1 of *Camera Lucida* and then subsides into his commentary in Part 2 on the 24 photographs he reproduces by Wessing, Klein, Nadar, Mapplethorpe, Kertész, and others. Barthes first introduces, briefly and tentatively, a succession of photographic concepts – adventure (19), animation (20), affect (21) – in order to arrive at his fundamental distinction between *studium* and *punctum*. These two concepts are not just means for him to deal with the phenomenological impact of photographs on him. They also enable him to understand how photography participates in an "infra-knowledge" (30) or episteme that is charged with desire. When we look, as Barthes did, at parental photographs, we are trying to satisfy our desire to know our parents as they were, just as looking at images of ourselves is part of our continuing project of coming to know who we are and what we have been.

The *studium* of a photograph is its subject of interest. Thus, photographs of buildings might appeal to my interest in architecture, or Victorian images might engage my historical curiosity. The studium is a matter of taste or commitment. It facilitates my cultural participation in the subject matter of a photograph (26). The *punctum*, on the other hand, "punctuates" the studium (26). It is a detail in the photograph that wounds, pricks, or marks the spectator (26). Although not the principal subject of the image, the punctum changes how one reads a photograph. The impact of the punctum is "brief and active" (49); and, like Lacan's gaze, it emanates from the picture to the viewer. It is an "insistent gaze" (49), an "off-center detail," a "symptom of disturbance" (51). The punctum is often best revealed from memory, after the fact, in order to recover its latency (53). Finally, the punctum is an "addition" to the photograph, not only in the sense that it is other than the main subject (like the two nuns in Wessing's photograph of military action in Nicaragua) but also in the sense that it seems to be what the spectator adds to the image even though it is in fact already there (55).

Barthes concludes *Camera Lucida* with a warning about two ways photographs get defused or tamed of what is explosive or threatening in them. One way is to turn photography into an art by giving prominence to the photographer and to photography's rivalry with painting. Here the analogy with literature would be in taming a text by treating it as a work whose significance is strictly limited by authorial intentionality.[19] The other means of trivializing the photograph is to allow photography to tyrannize over all other images and even over all other cultural forms. In the United States, Barthes observes, "only images exist and are produced and are consumed" (118). When this happens, photography loses its unique capacity to represent the real. Furthermore, a culture that allows itself to be ruled by its imaginary productions substitutes a fictionalized unity of itself for its real and potentially creative multiplicity. When photography asserts such multiplicity in the face of a culture's false, monolithic image of itself, one result is the repressive hysteria of those who attempted to close down exhibitions of Mapplethorpe's photographs and to punish the National Endowment for the Arts for supporting his work.[20]

The title of Barthes's book in its English version is taken from an image that recurs throughout his discussion of photography (especially 106–7). The camera lucida, which was invented in 1807, is a simple instrument consisting of a prism with four sides mounted on a stand above a piece of paper. By looking through the upper edge of the prism and down to the sheet of paper, the eye sees objects in front of the prism as though they are lying on the paper.[21] The purpose of the device is to be able to trace an image of real objects accurately onto the sheet of paper. In practice this instrument is very difficult to use because the slightest movement of the eye (by as much as one-sixteenth of an inch) causes the light beam from the prism to miss the pupil of the eye. Nevertheless, what is most attractive to Barthes about this device is that it provides him with a metaphor of what he wants from photography. What he longs for is a sign that can be read as reality itself, or as he puts it, a sign on which the referent is laminated (4–5). Throughout Barthes's work in semiotics and narratology, he was in search of a way to overcome the signifying limitations of language and the fictionalizing restrictions of narrative. To write what is real and to read what is true are parallel desires that he believed photography could satisfy, even if the knowledge the medium offers is the startling immediacy of undialectical mortality.

Cremonini and Althusser

The English edition of Althusser's *Lenin and Philosophy* (1971) concludes with
an appendix that reprints two texts on painting, both of which were first
published in 1966: "A Letter on Art in Reply to André Daspre" and
"Cremonini, Painter of the Abstract." Although a number of writers – including Italo Calvino, Umberto Eco, Alberto Moravia, and Stephen Spender – have
been drawn to Cremonini's work. Althusser's essay is one of the most important studies of his paintings.[22] Cremonini is significant, Althusser argues,
because he disturbs our ordinary sense of subjects and objects. To see his
paintings properly requires a new kind of gaze, one that does not depend upon
a desire for or a disgust with objects. Rather than painting objects or places,
"Cremonini 'paints' the *relations* which bind the objects, places and times"
(230). He is, therefore, a painter of the abstract. Rather than being an abstract
painter, in the sense of being in search of "pure possibility" in new forms, he
is a painter of the "real abstract," in the sense of the actual relation between
human beings and their things. Cremonini's art makes heavy demands on his
viewers. It requires of them not only that they see new relations between
subjects and objects; it also requires that the viewer enter into such
relationships.

Cremonini's paintings, according to Althusser, call into question the aesthetics of creation and consumption and the basic ideology of modern art
criticism. That ideology conceives of the relation between artist and work as
consisting of a mysterious "subjectivity of the painter, who inscribes his
'creative project' in the ideal materiality of his 'creation'" (230). Like Barthes,
Althusser here works to undermine the unreflective assumption that artist and
work are stable entities bound by a recoverable intentionality. According to
Althusser, Cremonini too confronted this ideology with "the idea that the
'mystery' of the 'inwardness' of a painter, of his 'creative project,' is no more
than his work itself, that the relations between a painter and his 'work' are
nothing but the 'relations' that he 'paints'" (231).

Althusser claims that the sequence of the objects Cremonini painted points
to the critical orientation of his work and that he began with geological
formations moved on to vegetation and animals, and then painted human
subjects (231–4). In fact, the sequence of Cremonini's interests is not as neat
as Althusser claims. The catalogue for the 1971 exhibition at Galleria Giulia
in Rome, for example, dates 80 paintings completed between 1952 and 1968.
Paintings of rocks, vegetation, animals, and people were completed in no
discernible order during this period. Images of young women and of mothers

and children, for example, date from the early fifties, flanked by some of Cremonini's major geological paintings.[23]

Althusser seems quite willing to dispense with his suspect chronology, however, in order to emphasize the formal similarities among dissimilar objects in Cremonini's paintings. Far more synchronic than diachronic, Cremonini managed to uncover a common geological foundation in the life forms he painted. For example, such studies of rock formations as *Le pietre al mare* (1957) and *Le pietre insieme* (1959) are strikingly similar as formal compositions to his paintings of crouching cows (*Bovi accovacciati* [1956]) and articulated vegetation (*Articolazione vegetali* [1960]). Even his human figures are no less inherently geological formations, either in the sense that he reminds his viewers of the bone barely concealed by human flesh (*L'uomo che porta la carne* [1957]) or in the sense that he depicts even a mother and child looking out the window as though they are frozen, monumental figures sculpted by Henry Moore (*Alla finestra* [1967]). Such objectification of the human subject, which Lacan called *chosisme*,[24] leads to Cremonini's relentless critique of a further aspect of the usually unquestioned humanistic ideology of the visual arts. That ideology sustains the fiction that when I took at a painting, I am a stable human *subject* looking at a stable, identifiable *object*. Even if the *subject* of the artistic *object* (the painting) is a human being, I assume that I can identify that *subject* by reading the title of the picture.

The focal point of the humanist ideology, Althusser claims, is the human face, which is the distinguishing sign of the individual and the outward expression of subjectivity:

> The humanist-religious ideological function of the human face is to be the seat of the "soul," of subjectivity, and therefore the visible proof of the existence of the human *subject* with all the ideological force of the concept of the *subject* (the centre from which the "world" is organized, because the human subject is the centre of its world, as a perceiving subject, as an active "creative" subject, as a free subject and hence as responsible for its objects and their meanings. (238)

The human faces in Cremonini's paintings, however, are drained of expression; and they appear to be drawn from figures of stone, rather than from living models. Althusser is quick to point out that what characterizes these faces is deformation rather than deformity. They are not ugly; instead, they display "a determinate absence of form" (238). They are deformed in the sense that they lack any form of individuality, which is precisely what one expects of the human face: Cremonini's faces "are haunted by an absence: a purely negative absence, that of the humanist function which is refused them, and which they refuse" (239).

In the resolute abstraction of his paintings, especially in his turning the human face to stone, Cremonini makes it possible for us to know ourselves by means of a fully challenged and critically exposed ideology. Like Marx and other great revolutionary thinkers, Cremonini demonstrates in his painting that it is only by knowing the laws of one's slavery that concrete individuality can be achieved. In this respect, "every work of art is born of a project both aesthetic and ideological" (241), and the function of every work of art is to reveal the reality of the existing ideology by distancing the spectator from it. More than any other object, the work of art enters into the most intimate relation to ideology, which gives it a unique opportunity to serve as a critique of ideology or to be subsumed by it. In Althusser's judgment, great artists are those who mark their creative position, who take into account the historical effects of adopting that position, and who assume responsibility for its ideological and emerging epistemological consequences.

In "A Letter on Art to André Daspre," Althusser elaborates on this argument a bit more fully. There Althusser explicitly rejects equating art with ideology. This does not mean, however, that art is a form of knowledge or a substitute for it. Rather, he claims, art has a certain necessary relationship to knowledge, which is more a relationship of difference than of identity. Art's unique capacity is to make us see ("nous donner à voir"), to make us perceive, and to make us feel "something which *alludes* to reality" (222). The reality we are able to see by art is the ideology from which art is born, from which it "detaches" itself, but to which it continues to allude. By creating an "internal distance" within ideology, the arts make us perceive "the very ideology in which they are held" (223). There is, then a fundamental difference between art and science in the specific form in which they render their objects: Whereas art enables us to see, to perceive, and to feel, science enables us to know.

Foucault and Magritte

In 1968 Foucault published a short version of *Ceci n'est pas une pipe* in the journal *Les Cahiers du chemin*. That essay was reissued in 1973 as an expanded text in book form. The English edition, published ten years later, includes several illustrations and two admiring but subtly critical letters from Magritte to Foucault, which were written just a year before the painter's death.[25] It seems likely that, had Magritte lived, there would have been further exchanges with Foucault concerning words and images. Foucault's text, which in many ways is a playful reworking of *The Order of Things*, focuses on Magritte's image of a pipe with the meticulously written accompanying caption, "Ceci n'est pas une pipe." Magritte had variously entitled his painting (or allowed it to be titled) *The Use of Language* and *The Betrayal of Images* (1928–9), and it is ironic that the caption has eclipsed what are apparently the painting's actual titles.[26] Magritte produced several versions of this picture, including *The Air and the Song* (1964) and *The Two Mysteries* (1966), which was finished the year Foucault published *The Order of Things*.[27] Foucault concentrates his attention principally on *The Use of Language* and *The Two Mysteries*.

In 1929 Magritte also composed an aphoristic manifesto entitled "Words and Images" ("Les Mots et les images"), which provides the context for *The Use of Language* and indicates the appropriateness of the painting's alternate title. Not only is Magritte's text about words and images, it also consists itself of words and images: short, declarative sentences, followed by simple illustrations. Here are some examples that relate specifically to Foucault's argument:

[1] An object is not so possessed of its name that one cannot find for it another which suits it better. [There follows a simple drawing of a leaf with the label "le canon" (that is, "model" or "perfect example").]

[2] There are objects that do without a name. [There follows an unmistakable, unlabeled image of a rowboat.]

[7] An image can take the place of a word in a proposition. [There follows the hand-written sentence, "The (sun) is concealed by the clouds," where the word "sun" is replaced by an image of a sun that is clearly *not* concealed behind clouds.]

[9] Everything tends to make one think that there is little relation between an object and that which represents it. [There follows a simple drawing of two identical houses, one labeled "the real object" and the other "the represented object."]

[12] One sees differently the image and the words in a painting. [There follows the image of a flower with the word "mountain" written over it.]

[14] An object never performs the same function as its name or its image. [There follows a drawing of a horse, a canvas that presumably depicts that horse, and a man speaking the word "horse" as he looks away from the other two objects in the picture.][28]

Part of the brilliance of *The Use of Language* is that it simultaneously illustrates these six points. Although Foucault refers only obliquely to Magritte's manifesto in his commentary (38–9), what he writes deals thoroughly with the complex relationships between words and images that absorbed Magritte's attention throughout his adult life.

Foucault's text is divided into six numbered sections. Part 1 is entitled "Two Pipes," which refers to the image of the pipe and the word "pipe" in the caption of *The Use of Language*; to the two paintings, *The Use of Language*

(1928–9) and *The Two Mysteries* (1966), which seems to incorporate a version of the earlier painting; to the large pipe that appears to float above the easel and to the pipe in the framed picture in *The Two Mysteries*; and possibly to a pipe that could be smoked in contrast to either the image or word for pipe. Part 2 develops the idea (or metaphor) that Magritte's paintings are "unraveled calligrams." (A calligram is a text such as Apollinaire and E. E. Cummings often composed, in which the positions of the words on the page draw the object that the words in the text describe.) Foucault argues that especially Magritte's 1928–9 painting is "created from the fragments of an unraveled calligram" (22). (Magritte himself might be coyly alluding here to Apollinaire's "Fumées," in which the second stanza takes the form of a pipe.) Part 3 sets up a contrast between the paintings of Magritte and those of Klee and Kandinsky, based on the twofold distinction between paintings that assert a separation between words and images, thus excluding resemblance, and those that posit "an equivalence between the fact of resemblance and the affirmation of a representative bond" (34). Here the initially surprising thesis is that Magritte's painting, in contrast to Klee's and Kandinsky's, is "wedded to exact resemblances" (35). Part 4 confronts directly the relationships between word and image in Magritte's work and develops Foucault's major observation about Magritte's critique of traditional painting: "Magritte," he argues, "allows the old space of representation to rule, but only at the surface, no more than a polished stone, bearing words and shapes: beneath, nothing" (41). Part 5 develops this observation, reformulates it – "Magritte dissociated similitude from resemblance, and brought the former into play against the latter" (44) – and applies it to the pipe paintings. Finally, Part 6 summarizes the twofold argument of the book: that the principles constituting the fundamental tension in classical painting were the separation between sign and image and the equivalence of resemblance and affirmation; and that Magritte worked to recombine signs and images in order to reveal the void beneath them. Each of these sections of Foucault's book is highly playful in language, as suits his subject, although the book's argument also seriously recapitulates some of the major themes of Foucault's own work.

Foucault begins by referring to the multiplicity of Magritte's versions of the pipe, in which eventually the later ones, such as *The Two Mysteries*, incorporate or allude to the first version of 1928–9. Whereas the first version achieves its uncanny effects by its simplicity, the second works by the multiplication of ambiguity, since it is both a picture of a pipe and a picture of a picture of a pipe, despite or because of its caption of denial. The caption, strangely, is neither the title of the work nor exactly a part of the picture, and the range of its reference is ambiguous. It may refer to either of the two painted pipes or to both in relation to a model or idea of a pipe. In his May 23, 1966 letter to Foucault, Magritte distinguishes between resemblance and similitude in the context of arguing that painting is a mode of thought. "Things," he asserts, "do not have resemblances, they do or do not have similitudes." He goes on to argue that "Only thought resembles. It resembles by being what it sees, hears, or knows; it becomes what the world offers it" (57).[29] Thus there is similitude between the two pipes in the painting in terms of shape, position, and color. But the caption engenders precisely the kind of perceptual doubt that is a legacy of Descartes and Hume and that has the potential of raising what we think about the pipe or pipes to the level of knowledge. In both Magritte's paintings and Foucault's commentary there may be a specific, ironic allusion to Descartes's Third Meditation, where questions about the reliability of perception, the existence of God, and the power of skeptical thought to ground existence all come together. The connection here is Foucault's (and possibly Magritte's) pun on the French saying "le nom d'une pipe," which is a substitute for the exclamation, "for God's sake." Once we begin to wonder what the relationships might be between the two painted pipes, between both those pipes and the word "pipe" in the caption, between the 1928–9 and the 1966 paintings, and between any of these versions of pipes and one that might be smoked, we have moved from similitude to resemblance, where thought takes place and where the stakes get very high.[30]

The strangeness of the first version of the pipe (*The Use of Language*) lies not in the surface contradiction between word and image so much as in what Barthes (by way of Sartre) might have called their intentional structure. The "academic" simplicity of the image allows "the object it represents to appear without hesitation or equivocation" (20). In this sense the image asserts that it *is* a pipe. In that sense Magritte's painting could do without a title, unlike, for example, Klee's *The Wild Man* (1922).[31] Perhaps even Cremonini's crouching cows, because of their initial similitude to geological forms, benefit from a title, as though to produce in thought the resonance of resemblance. Each of these pictures in its own way rejects any easy identification among image, word, and object.

Foucault seizes upon the metaphor of an "unraveled calligram" in order to get at the precise relation between word and image in Magritte's painting. The calligram, Foucault explains, has a triple role:

to augment the alphabet, to repeat something without the aid of rhetoric, to trap things in a double cipher. First it brings a text and a shape as close together as possible. It is composed of lines delimiting the form of an object while also arranging the sequence of letters. It lodges statements in the space of a shape, and makes the text *say* what the drawing *represents*. (20–1)

The ultimate aim of the calligram, then, is to show and to name at once, thus overcoming "the oldest opposition of our alphabetical civilization." In its fusion of word and image, the calligram is an occasion for reading and looking at the same time. Like Barthes's metaphor of the photograph as a camera lucida, Foucault's calligram is a means of overcoming the sign's displacement and deferral of the real. But the calligram too is an image that invokes as much difference as resemblance. For Foucault it is not just that Magritte's drawings are calligrams–or even unraveled calligrams – rather, they seem "to be created from the fragments of an unraveled calligram" (22). Although Apollinaire was one of Magritte's favorite writers (60n), Magritte has nothing to say about calligrams in his manifesto "Words and Images."[32] What Foucault wants from the metaphor of the unraveled calligram is that in saying what it wants to say twice (by words and images made of words) the calligram positively achieves what Magritte produces negatively, as a double paradox: at the moment when the caption "should reveal the name" of the object in the painting, it denies "that the object is what it is " (24). Thus, the potential for calligraphic double assertion is unraveled and turned into the double paradox that the simple and declarative forms of the image and the orthography undermine each other. Another, perhaps unanticipated, twist of Magritte's irony here (possibly its third paradox) is that the title of his painting – *The Use of Language*–has been supplanted by the caption. Curiously, Foucault often refers to the caption as "the title" (e.g. 36), as though he too had succumbed to Magritte's irony.

In order to give a historical sense of Magritte's achievement, Foucault briefly contrasts his work with that of Kandinsky and Klee, whose theories of painting lacked the philosophical precision of Magritte's, however much they shared a common ambition for painting to deal as directly as possible with the real. For example, Kandinsky, apparently under the influence of his studies in theosophy, tried to develop a universal grammar of visual forms that would reveal symbolic emotional equivalents between forms and emotions. "Modern art," he insisted, "can only be born when signs become symbols."[33] Whereas Kandinsky longed to fix the symbolic resemblances of forms and colors to specific emotions in order to stabilize the language of painting, Klee wanted to look behind visible things to uncover a hidden reality that he could grasp in paint. Thus in 1920 he wrote, "Formerly we used to represent things visible on earth, things we either liked to look at or would have liked to see. Today we reveal the reality that is behind visible things, thus expressing the belief that the visible world is merely an isolated case in relation to the universe and that there are many more other, latent realities."[34] Foucault sees the ambitions of Klee, Kandinsky, and Magritte as important responses to two principles that have, he believed, ruled Western painting since the fifteenth century.

One principle is the separation of images, which imply resemblance, from signs, which in their arbitrary relationship to what they signify deny resemblance. According to this principle, the sign and the image always preserve their distinctness. Rather than merging or intersecting, either one rules alone or dominates the other. In such paintings as *Villa R* (1919), however, Klee abolished this principle.[35] As Foucault puts it, in Klee's work "boats, houses, persons are at the same time recognizable figures and elements of writing." Thus Klee affects "the intersection, within the same medium, of representation by resemblance and of representation by signs" (33–4). The other principle is the equivalence between resemblance and representational affirmation. When a figure resembles an object or another figure, it silently makes the statement, " 'What you see is *that*' " (34). According to this principle, resemblance and affirmation are indissociable. However, by treating lines and colors as things that are on an equal footing with ordinary objects, Kandinsky set out to rupture this principle in such paintings as *White Balancing* (1944) and *Improvisation: Green Center* (1935).[36]

In his first letter to Foucault, Magritte would seem to dismiss Klee and Kandinsky with a stroke of his pen:

> There is no reason to accord more importance to the invisible than to the visible, nor vice versa. What does not "lack" importance is the mystery evoked *in fact* by the visible and the invisible, and which can be evoked *in principle* by the thought that unites "things" in an order that evokes mystery. (57)

As Foucault points out, Magritte is so committed to exact resemblance that he has the leaf and the tree or the ship and the sea take on the forms of each other in *L'Incendie* and *Le Séducteur*.[37] Although Magritte's methods are opposed to those of Klee and Kandinsky, his project – which is to separate radically the sign and the image and thus to challenge that two principles that Foucault sees as fundamental to the ideology of Western art – is nevertheless complementary to theirs. Whereas Klee and Kandinsky believed that they could simply step outside those principles, set them aside, or banish them, Magritte thought it necessary to work through in order to get beyond them. Having so carefully studied in *The Order of Things* the historical hold of those principles on Western culture since the Renaissance, Foucault champions Magritte's procedure and affirms its philosophical commitment and significance.

Far from denigrating either the sign or the image, Magritte and Foucault were committed to a positive critical examination of both language and painting in order to understand their differing holds on how we think and know.[38] Here, as always for Foucault, such a critical project is an affirmative endeavor, which he sees as the most important legacy of the Enlightenment. Critique in this sense is "a historical investigation into the events that have led us to constitute ourselves and to recognize ourselves as subjects of what we are doing, thinking, saying."[39]

The temptation to rush to read the title of a painting that one sees for the first time is difficult to resist. Magritte, however, confesses that his titles "are chosen in such a way as to keep anyone from assigning [his] paintings to the familiar region that habitual thought appeals to in order to escape perplexity" (36). Like the caption, "Ceci n'est pas une pipe," Magritte's titles perplex in the interest of bringing the act of naming into critical focus in an effort to make us reflect on the desire to still such perplexity in language. Magritte's caption, Foucault argues, both reveals how far discourse penetrates into the form of things and how its power is simultaneously the ability to allure, to deny, and to redouble (37). That Magritte's and Foucault's projects were parallel critical endeavors is perhaps clearest in Magritte's modest statement of his creative purpose, which Foucault quotes with obvious approval: "Between words and objects one can create new relations and specify characteristics of language and objects generally ignored in everyday life" (38).

Foucault's most important observation about Magritte's art is his recognition that first he creates a visual space in which every formal detail appears to be governed by the principle of resemblance and representation; second, he surreptitiously and ironically reintroduces the linguistic sign into that visual space; third, he allows the disorder that results from the sign's intrusion on the space of the obsessively ordered image to play itself out, which in turn reveals the "filmy thinness" of objects. Whereas Klee thought he could simply create a new space for the plastic signs he invented, Magritte more radically allows the shallowly buried void that is momentarily hidden beneath the marble solidity of traditional art's representational surface to erupt. Of that "old space of representation," Foucault writes that "It is a gravestone" (41). Like Barthes's *eidos* of the photograph, the rupturing force that Foucault witnesses Magritte release into modern painting is the reality of death that traditional painting has attempted to entomb beneath the funeral slab of representation. The most aggressive version of death's eruption into representation in his work is Magritte's posthumously cast sculpture based on his own painting entitled *Perspective: David's "Madame Récamier."* In his painting Magritte substituted a reclining coffin for David's Madame Récamier. Although Magritte died before the project was complete, his designs for the sculpture nevertheless led to the production of the several objects in the painting, which are the actual size of pieces of furniture, carefully modelled on David's painting. The coffin on the couch was cast from a specially designed wooden model of an actual coffin.[40] Here the real profoundly intrudes upon Magritte's ironic representational affirmation.

Foucault concludes his book by arguing that Magritte not only broke the bond between resemblance and affirmation but also dissociated similitude from resemblance, thus freeing painting from the two principles that had dominated it since the Renaissance. As he looks at *The Two Mysteries*, which for him epitomizes Magritte's achievement, Foucault hears in the painting a conversation taking place among seven voices: First, the pipe in the painting on the easel says that it is not a pipe but a drawing that relates to the other pipe in terms of simple similitude. Second, the pipe above the easel echoes the voice of the pipe in the frame: it too, though neither in a frame nor on an easel, is not a pipe but merely a painted similitude. Third, the caption also says of itself that it is not a pipe but merely a "graphism that resembles only itself" (48). Fourth, bound by the frame, the caption and the lower pipe, asserting the combined power of signs and images, reject the abstract, floating apparition of pipe. Fifth, the two pipes, bound by their communal similitude, reject the written statement, which in no way resembles a pipe, composed as the caption is of arbitrary signs. Finally, the dislocated voice of one or both of the paintings says that both pipes and the caption are but different forms of simulation. Together these seven voices – and Magritte's art as a whole – restore to itself the similitude of objects.

Although their procedures and investigative materials are radically different, Barthes, Althusser, and Foucault followed the same critical path as Lacan, Derrida, and Kristeva. They all worked from within the arbitrariness and instability of language in an effort to find in its plurivocity and multiple signification an opening into the real. For all of them, the image was a key to such a discovery because it operates in language as metaphor but outside it as well, in visual perception, in photography and painting, and in the imago's hold on the future of the human subject. Furthermore, they were all convinced that the visual and verbal arts have the capacity to reveal the truth about the human condition as a form of knowledge that is available nowhere else.

Notes

1 For a systematic survey of the literature on such metaphors as these, see Martin Jay, *Downcast Eyes: The Denigration of Vision in Twentieth-century*

French Thought (Berkeley: University of California Press, 1993), esp. pp. 1–20.

2	*Camera Lucida*, trans. Richard Howard (London: Harper Collins, 1984). All references to this book are given by page numbers in parentheses.

3	For an account of Barthes's illness and the intellectual significance of the student community in the sanatorium, see Louis-Jean Calvet, *Roland Barthes: A Biography*, trans. Sarah Wykes (Oxford: Polity Press, 1994), pp. 45–69.

4	"Présentation des 'Temps modernes.'" Reprinted in *Situations II* (Paris, 1948), p. 16.

5	*The Psychology of Imagination* (New York: Citadel Press), p. 27.

6	The importance of Husserl's *Ideas* for Sartre is even clearer in *Imagination: A Psychological Critique*, trans. Forrest Williams (Ann Arbor: Michigan University Press, 1962), esp. pp. 127–44.

7	Pp. 28–30.

8	Pp. 30–1.

9	Pp. 30–2.

10	For a note on the curious publishing history of Lacan's paper, see *Reading Theory*, pp. 27, 100n.

11	For a detailed account of Lacan's paper, see *Reading Theory*, pp. 26–34.

12	This theory is elaborated in *Four Fundamental Concepts of Psychoanalysis*. For a commentary, see *Reading Theory*, pp. 214–17.

13	"The Great Family of Man," in *Mythologies*, trans. Annette Lavers (New York: Hill and Wang, 1972), pp. 100–2.

14	*The Family of Man* (New York: Museum of Modern Art, 1955), p. 2.

15	Quoted by Barthes in "The Great Family of Man," p. 100.

16	"The Great Family of Man," p. 101.

17	Ibid.

18	"The Photographic Image," in *Image – Music – Text*, trans. Stephen Heath (London: Fontana, 1977), p. 17.

19	See "From Work to Text," in *Image – Music – Text*, pp. 155–64.

20	See Wendy Steiner, *The Scandal of Pleasure* (Chicago: University of Chicago Press, 1995).

21	W. H. Wollaston, "Description of the Camera Lucida, "*Nicholson's Journal*, 17 (1807), p. 12.

22	For a brief assessment of Cremonini's later work, see Ronny Cohen, "Leonardo Cremonini," *Artforum*, 26 (1987), p. 139.

23	Enrico Vallecchi, *80 designi di Cremonino* (Rome: Galleria Giulia, 1971) [unpaginated exhibition catalogue]. A conversation with Althusser and Cremonini was published in *Démocratie Nouvelle* in 1967.

24	"The Freudian Thing," in *Écrits*, trans. Alan Sheridan (London: Tavistock, 1977), esp. pp. 117–24. Cf. Martin Heidegger, "The Thing," in *Poetry, Language, Thought*, trans. Albert Hofstadter (New York: Harper and Row, 1971), pp. 127, 168.

25 *This Is Not a Pipe*, trans. James Harkness (Berkeley: University of California Press, 1983). All references to this text appear as page numbers in parentheses.

26 Foucault consistently mis-titles the painting and dates it as 1926, instead of 1928–9.

27 There is a generous selection of reproductions of the various pipe paintings in Suzi Gablik, *Magritte* (Greenwich, CT: New York Graphic Society, 1970), plates 109–12.

28 René Magritte, "Les Mots et les images," *La Révolution surréaliste*, 5 : 12 (1929), trans. Suzi Gablik, *Magritte*, pp. 138–40. I have numbered the seventeen aphorisms for reference purposes.

29 Silvano Levy, "Foucault on Magritte on Resemblance," *MLR*, 85 (1990), pp. 50–6, stresses the changes in Foucault's thinking since *The Order of Things* about similitude and resemblance under the impact of Magritte's letters and other writings on this topic. For a good discussion of Magritte's language pictures, see Uwe M. Schneede, *René Magritte: Life and Work* (New York: Barron's, 1982), pp. 35–46.

30 The final illustration in Le Corbusier's *Towards a New Architecture* (Paris: Éditions Crès, 1923) is a briar pipe. The argument of the book's final chapter is that new architecture can make it possible to avoid social revolution. On the importance of this illustration for Magritte, see Robert Hughes, *The Shock of the New* (New York: Knopf, 1981), pp. 243–4.

31 Plate 10.

32 The closest he comes is aphorism 11: "In a painting the words are of the same substance as the image" (Gablik, *Magritte*, p. 139).

33 Quoted by Hughes, p. 301.

34 Quoted by Hughes, p. 304.

35 Plate 9.

36 Plates 11 and 12.

37 Plates 13 and 14.

38 Here I disagree with the thesis of Martin Jay's excellent book *Downcast Eyes*. Jay sees himself as a defender of the "Enlightenment faith" (p. 17) in illumination against Barthes, Althusser, Foucault, Deleuze, and others who, Jay, believes, denigrate it. Jay seems to think that critical examination is a form of denigration.

39 "What Is Enlightenment?" in Paul Rabinow (ed.), *Foucault Reader* (New York: Pantheon, 1984), p. 46.

40 Gablik, *Magritte*, p. 181.

8

Deleuze: Philosophy, Psychoanalysis, and Capitalism

One of the most difficult obstacles to overcome in reading texts by contemporary French theorists and philosophers is the proliferation of synthetic caricatures of what they have written or what they are presumed to have written. For example, to homogenize Lacan, Foucault, Derrida, Barthes, Althusser, Kristeva, Irigaray, and Deleuze under such labels as "poststructuralism" or (worse yet) "postmodernism" is immediately to obscure not only the distinctiveness of the thought of each of them but also to forget the importance they attach to difference and to careful reading. When Lacan reads Freud, Derrida reads Heidegger, Althusser reads Marx, Foucault reads Nietzsche, or Kristeva reads Hegel, they each proceed with painstaking care. They are all that rare sort of reader whom Nietzsche so prized, the slow reader who searches not for a reification of experience that he or she has already had, but for an opening into the possibility of a new kind of thought or experience. It may be, however, that these thinkers unwittingly invite a synthetic misperception of their differing projects because each of them is responding (however distinctively) to certain fundamental, inescapable questions, such as: What (or who) is a human subject (or person)? How does language (or writing) function in relation to human subjects? What does what we know of subjects and language require of us as moral or political agents? What, therefore, is philosophy's relationship to psychoanalysis and to economics? Another reason for their being so often infelicitously lumped together is that, for example, Lacan, Derrida, Kristeva, Foucault, Barthes, Althusser, and Deleuze have written in response to some of the same texts – especially those of Marx, Nietzsche, and Freud – and that they have read (and have often reviewed) each other's work with meticulous critical attention.

There is not only considerable critical diversity in contemporary French thought, there is also within each thinker extensive *multiplicity*, to use one of Deleuze's key words. For Deleuze, to affirm multiplicity is to be an empiricist or a pluralist, one, first of all, who is convinced that the abstract does not itself explain anything but waits itself to be explained and, secondly, one who is determined to find the creative circumstances that make possible the production of something new, rather than being determined to find what is eternal or universal.[1] The writing produced by the empirical, pluralistic, multiplicitous thinker is therefore distinctive. In his book entitled *Dialogues*, Deleuze argues that the minimum real unit of writing

> is not the word, the idea, the concept or the signifier, but the *assemblage*. It is always an assemblage which produces utterances. Utterances do not have as their cause a subject who would act as a subject of enunciation, any more than they are related to subjects as subjects of utterance. The utterance is the product of an assemblage – which is always collective, which brings into play within us and outside us populations, multiplicities, territories, becomings, affects, events. The proper name does not designate a subject, but something which happens, at least between two terms which are not subjects, but agents, elements. Proper names are not names of persons, but of peoples and tribes, flora and fauna, military operations or typhoons, collectives, limited companies and production studios. The author is a subject of enunciation but the writer – who is not an author – is not. The writer invents assemblages starting from assemblages which have invented him, he makes one multiplicity pass into another.[2]

Here Deleuze is appropriating a term from surrealist art, where an *assemblage* is usually a three-dimensional montage of ready-made materials. Since he thinks of the writer as a multiplicity who invents assemblages, it is not surprising that so many of Deleuze's texts are collaborative productions, several of these, the most important, with Félix Guattari. What is universal in these assemblages, however, is that the collaborations are virtually seamless, leaving little or no trace of where Deleuze's thought merges with his collaborator's. Thus, to read Deleuze is to encounter texts – "Deleuzo-guattarian"[3] texts – that are assemblages to which his name cannot be definitively affixed. Furthermore, to conceive of the writer of these texts is to imagine not a fixed, individuated authorial authority but a duet and eventually a chorus of voices.

As might be expected, the difficult part in producing such assemblages, whether co-written or not, "is making all the elements of a non-homogeneous set converge, making them function together." Again in *Dialogues*, Deleuze argues that

> Structures are linked to conditions of homogeneity, but assemblages are not. The assemblage is co-functioning, it is "sympathy", symbiosis. With deepest sympathy. Sympathy is not a vague feeling of respect or of spiritual participation: on the contrary, it is the exertion or the penetration of bodies, hatred or

love, for hatred is also a compound, it is a body, it is no good except when it is compounded with what it hates. Sympathy is bodies who love or hate each other, each time with populations in play, in these bodies or on these bodies. Bodies may be physical, biological, psychic, social, verbal: they are always bodies or corpora. The author, as subject of enunciation, is first of all a spirit: sometimes he identifies with his characters or makes us identify with them, or with the idea which they represent; sometimes, on the other hand, he introduces a distance which allows him and us to observe, to criticize, to prolong. But this is no good. The author creates a world, but there is no world which awaits us to be created. Neither identification nor distance, neither proximity nor remoteness, for, in all these cases, one is led to speak for, in the place of . . . One must, on the contrary, speak *with*, write *with*. With the world, with a part of the world, with people. Not a talk at all, but a conspiracy, a collision of love or hatred. . . . This is assembling, being in the middle, on the line of encounter between an internal world and the external world.[4]

What is most remarkable about this passage – and in this sense it is emblematic of Deleuze's philosophical style – is that it oscillates between the impersonal and the personal, between the remote and the intimate: Human beings are functional multiplicities who produce assemblages when they write; but their assemblages arise out of sympathy, love, and a desire to speak with and write with others. To assemble, then, is to mediate between the internal world of thought and the external world of moral and political action.

But to think this way about oneself and others is disconcerting. It requires at first a defamiliarization of oneself, even a questioning of whether referring to oneself as *one* may not be an effort to conceal the multiplicity that is each human subject and, accordingly, to defer the recognition of the assemblage that is the written text. Perhaps we have wrapped ourselves in a comfortable, humanistic identity-mythology in order to avoid the realization that we are desiring-machines. In order to divest us of that mythology, to defamiliarize us from ourselves, to bring us to a full realization of human multiplicity, the language of the opening sentences of Deleuze and Guattari's *Anti-Oedipus* is almost violent; it is also purposefully paranoiac:

> It is at work everywhere, functioning smoothly at times, at other times in fits and starts. It breathes, it heats, it eats. It shits and fucks. What a mistake to have ever said *the* id. Everywhere *it* is machines – real ones, not figurative ones: machines driving other machines, machines being driven by other machines, with all the necessary couplings and connections. An organ-machine is plugged into an energy-source-machine: the one produces a flow that the other interrupts. The breast is a machine that produces milk, and the mouth a machine coupled to it.[5]

This image of the anti-Oedipal, non-ego-unified, unindividuated human being is itself an assemblage made up of the scene of the infernal machine at the end of Beckett's *Malone Dies*, Wilhelm Reich's Orgone machine, Dali's and Lacan's theories of paranoiac knowledge, Samuel Butler's "The Book of the Machines," and Richard Lindner's painting, *Boy with Machine*, which "shows a huge, pudgy, bloated boy working one of his little desiring-machines, after having hooked it up to a vast technical social machine." Making such connections, Deleuze and Guattari insist, "is what even the very young child does."[6]

At first it may seem surprising to discover that Deleuze was such a careful historian of philosophy, given his conceptions of multiplicity and assemblage. Like Michel Foucault, however, Deleuze was inspired by Nietzsche to be suspicious of the search for origins and definitive outcomes, which often determines the course of historical investigation. Although Deleuze wrote meticulous, classic studies of Hume, Nietzsche, Kant, Bergson, Spinoza, and Foucault, he is more a genealogist than a historian of philosophy. Foucault, in his commentary on Nietzsche's historiography, pointed out that genealogy reveals the heterogenous systems of thought that are masked by the idea of the self, systems of thought that purposefully and productively inhibit the formation of any fixed form of identity. Whereas Foucault, in such books as *The Order of Things* and *The History of Sexuality*, explored large and powerful epistemic structures that shape such disciplines as linguistics, biology, and economics, Deleuze examines the smaller units of thought that travel under such proper names as Kant and Spinoza.

The best study of Deleuze as a historian (or genealogist) of philosophy, it seems to me, is Foucault's "Theatrum Philosophicum," which starts out as a review of two books by Deleuze: *Difference and Repetition* and *The Logic of Sense*. Although he announces that it is his intention to follow the various paths that lead to the heart of Deleuze's books, Foucault quickly admits that the metaphor of the heart is misleading. There is no heart or center, but instead a problem or a decentering. (Deleuze later champions the metaphor of the rhizome, that subterranean stem that emits roots and shoots.) Rather than a fixed point of return or the sense of a definitive sphere, Deleuze's texts offer "a distribution of notable points."[7] In fact (Deleuze argues and Foucault agrees) the history of philosophy is a history of attempts to overturn Platonism. If philosophy is "any attempt, regardless of its source" to reverse Platonism, then philosophy begins with Plato at the conclusion of his dialogue the *Sophist*, where it is virtually impossible to distinguish between Socrates himself and his Sophistic imitators; or it begins with the Sophists, who attempted to stifle the rise of Platonism with their ridicule of its greatness; or it begins with

Aristotle's turning away from his teacher, as, for example, in those chilling lines of the *Ethics* (I: 6), where Aristotle announces that although Plato is dear to him, "it is our sacred duty to honor truth more highly than friends."

Plato, in Foucault's elegant summary, "is said to have opposed essence to appearance, a higher world to this terrestrial world, the sun of truth to the shadows of the cave (and it becomes our duty to bring essences back into the world, to glorify the world, and to place the sun of truth within man)"; but Deleuze instead discovers Plato's uniqueness in his divisions, in "the delicate sorting operation which precedes the discovery of essence, because it necessitates the world of essences in its separation of false simulacra from the multitude of appearances."[8] Deleuze sees philosophy's reversal of Platonism as first an insidious displacement of itself within Platonism, then as a descent to those gestures and methods that would exclude the simulacrum – as, for example, Aristotle's insistence that for the good to be the good it must be attainable – then as an encouragement of those voices that Platonism has excluded; then as the construction of a "dethroned para-Platonism," which would be a simulacrum of a critique of the simularcrum. Thus humor replaces Socratic irony; Plato is perverted; and philosophy becomes professional. The great and current challenge to philosophy is to carry out a thorough critique of those phantasms that philosophy has allowed to become the illusory substance of metaphysics. Philosophy cannot allow itself any longer to be mesmerized by phantasms. That is what psychoanalysis has done, and for that reason it should be understood as a metaphysical practice that concerns itself with phantasms, which is why psychoanalysis so closely parallels theatre.

Before turning to Deleuze's critique of psychoanalysis, we might add one further observation about his advocacy of multiplicity, difference, division, and philosophy's reversal of Platonism. When he was a student at the Sorbonne in the mid-1940s, Deleuze scrupulously studied Hegel, Husserl, and the early Heidegger and was especially influenced – as was Foucault – by Jean Hyppolite's mediation of their thought. After he left the Sorbonne, however, it seemed to Deleuze that, without knowing it at the time, he and his fellow students "were strangely trapped in the history of philosophy" and that their devotion to Hegel, Husserl, and Heidegger amounted to "a scholasticism worse than that of the Middle Ages."[9] Like Derrida, who took a similar turn much later, Deleuze was drawn to certain "anti-rationalist" thinkers (as he called them) who had managed to escape the history of philosophy while at the same time being part of it. Thus, in amazingly quick succession, Deleuze published major studies of Hume (1953), Lucretius (1961), Nietzsche (1962), Bergson (1966), and Spinoza (1968), all before his collaboration with Guattari began. It is especially Deleuze's highly influential work on Nietzsche that lays the foundation for that later work. Indeed, it appears that Deleuze's *Nietzsche and Philosophy* was already finished when Heidegger's *Nietzsche* was published in 1961. (Heidegger's massive interpretive defense against Nietzsche, though delivered as lectures much earlier, was not translated into French until 1971.) Thus Deleuze's book, which celebrates Nietzsche as a serious and systematic thinker, is partially but significantly responsible for the kind of careful, sustained attention given to Nietzsche in France since its publication in 1962, especially in the writings of Derrida, Foucault, Klossowski, Blanchot, Kofman, and Irigaray.

Although there is no reason to suppose that he was possessively concerned about the priority of his work, it now seems clear that Deleuze was in certain ways a genealogist before Foucault and a deconstructionist before Derrida. In his fine commentary on Nietzsche and genealogy, Deleuze delineates the distinctive features of genealogy: It signifies both the value of origin and the origin of values; it is opposed to both absolute and to relative or utilitarian values; it affirms the differential element in values in the sense of demanding that the assertion of values be critically grounded; it uncovers the suspect origin of values and recognizes in them the mixture of the noble and the base, the altruistic and the opportunistic; it affirms critique as positive action and not as defensive reaction; it recognizes that, rather than destroying all value, critique imbues values with life.[10] (Foucault's essay "Nietzsche, Genealogy, History" did not appear until nine years after Deleuze's book.) Just as genealogy's critique of values grounds rather than destroys them, so does deconstruction's critique of structure ground rather than destroy signification. Whether the structure being explored is a written text or the history of philosophy, deconstructive reading investigates so thoroughly the otherwise neglected micro-structures of texts as to find hidden crevices or fissures that are always already there in human structures and that have the potential of opening up those structures to what they may defensively want to exclude from themselves. These openings, which are where critique does its most effective work, are also pervasive instances of what Deleuze calls difference and Derrida *différance*. Deleuze sees philosophy as being born in one such crevice: that point where Platonism begins to reverse itself. Derrida carries Deleuze's critique of Platonism further by seeing writing, which Plato disparaged in the *Phaedrus*, as the prime manifestation of difference. (Derrida's manifesto for deconstruction – "Structure, Sign, and Play in the Discourse of the Human Sciences" [1966] – was delivered at Johns Hopkins University four years after *Nietzsche and Philosophy*. Deleuze, nevertheless, was in turn influenced by Derrida, especially in his book *Difference and Repetition* [1968].)

When Deleuze and Guattari published their controversial critique of psychoanalysis and Marxism – *Anti-Oedipus: Capitalism and Schizophrenia* – in 1972, Lacan's international reputation was at its height. Guattari, beginning in 1953, had attended Lacan's seminars, had been analyzed by Lacan, had become (as a practicing analyst himself) a professional member of Lacan's École Freudienne de Paris, and had made extensive use of Lacan's readings of Freud in his own publications. Lacan's project had been to rescue Freud from such professional organizations as the International Psychoanalytic Association, which in its efforts to systematize and to promote Freud's thought had succeeded in stifling it. Furthermore, Lacan was determined to rescue Freud from himself. One side of Freud he saw as the fearless explorer of the depths of the unconscious. But there was also another side that was a self-promoter, an advocate of the ego, and a salesman for psychoanalysis. By concentrating his attention on Freud's poetics, on his argument by metaphor, and on his admirable capacity for self-criticism, Lacan had hoped to bring about a return to what was best in Freud and to turn attention away from such synthetic books as Freud's *An Outline of Psychoanalysis* and toward such speculative texts as *Beyond the Pleasure Principle*. Lacan's project was clearly of major importance to Deleuze and Guattari, although they go even further in their critique of psychoanalysis than Lacan was willing to go. Unlike Lacan, they were convinced that Freud had irredeemably betrayed the significance of his own investigations into the unconscious. Having exposed the id, Freud was determined to put the ego in its place; and having discovered the power of the unconscious to generate the multiplicities of the human subject, he developed the repressive discourses of psychoanalysis to tame his discovery. Lacan, Deleuze, and Guattari focus considerable attention on one sentence in the *New Introductory Lectures on Psychoanalysis*: "Wo es war, soll Ich werden," which is best translated as "Where id was, there ego shall be." This sentence is emblematic, for Deleuze and Guattari, of the two fatal flaws in psychoanalysis: "that it breaks up all productions of desire and crushes all formations of utterances."[11] Despite its relentless determination to become the master discourse about human beings, psychoanalysis has displayed its cowardice in the face of its own most creative discoveries. It has come to speak for and as the ego. Freud put the matter simply but positively when he wrote, "Psycho-analysis is an instrument to enable the ego to achieve a progressive conquest of the id" (SE, XIX: 56).

Deleuze's first criticism of psychoanalysis is that the Freudian formula needs to be reversed: Neither the unconscious nor the id is a place, despite Freud's referring to them as "localizations" (SE, XXIII: 145). The only "where" that the id was or the ego shall be is a certain place in Freud's theoretical writings. The unconscious does not produce us; we produce it. Far from being ruled by repressed memories or phantasms of childhood that under analysis we later reconstruct, we produce instead "blocs of child-becoming with *blocs of childhood* which are always in the present."[12] It is not with slips of the tongue or puns or dreams that we produce the unconscious, Deleuze insists; rather, "the unconscious is a substance to be manufactured, to get flowing – a social and political space to be conquered."[13] Furthermore, Freud and Lacan were mistaken to think that we are subjects and objects of desire or subjects of enunciation:

> Fluxes are the only objectivity of desire itself. Desire is the system of a-signifying signs with which fluxes of the unconsicious are produced in a social field. There is no blossoming of desire, wherever it happens – in an unremark-able [that is, non-Oedipal] family or a local school – which does not call established structures into question. Desire is revolutionary because it always wants more connections and assemblages. But psychoanalysis cuts off and beats down all connections, all assemblages – it hates desire, it hates politics.[14]

Deleuze's point here is that psychoanalysis has fundamentally misunderstood human beings by failing to recognize their multiplicity. Or, worse yet, psychoanalysis was on the way to understanding the multiplicity of human beings when it became terrified by its discovery of the power for division that resides in the id. Psychoanalysis then proceeded to hide what it had discovered by committing itself to empowering the ego over the id, thus turning the language of psychoanalysis into a discourse of repression.

Deleuze's second criticism is that psychoanalysis has not only misunderstood language but has "prevented the formation of utterances" (79). In their content,

> assemblages . . . are populated by becomings and intensities, by intensive circu-lations, by various multiplicities (packs, masses, species, races, populations, tribes . . .). And in their expression, assemblages handle indefinite articles or pronouns which are not at all indeterminate ("a" tummy, "some" people, "one" hits "a" child . . .) – verbs in the infinitive which are not undifferentiated but which mark processes (to walk, to kill, to love . . .) – proper names which are not people but events (they can be groups, animals, entities, singularities, collec-tives, everything that is written with a capital letter . . .).[15]

For all Freud's philological fastidiousness, psychoanalysis, according to Deleuze, fails to understand the indefinite article, the infinitive of the verb, and the proper name. Thus, when one of Melanie Klein's child analysands speaks about a tummy, Klein hears only "my mummy's tummy"; or when the child asks how people grow up, she hears "Will I be big like my daddy?"

Deleuze cites similar efforts at overdetermination from Freud's case studies: Although the "wolf man" talks to Freud about six or seven wolves, Freud wants to hear about only one that might represent the father. Similarly, in his treatment of little Hans, Freud

> takes no account of the assemblage (building-street-nextdoor-warehouse-omnibus-horse-a-horse-falls-is-whipped!); he takes no account of the situation (the child had been forbidden to go into the street, etc.); he takes no account of little Hans's animal-becoming, the infinitive as marker of a becoming, because every other way out has been blocked up: the childhood bloc, the bloc of Hans's animal-becoming, the infinitive as marker of a becoming, the line of flight or the movement of deterritorialization). The only important thing for Freud is that the horse be the father – and that's the end of it.[16]

Psychoanalysis puts a code in the place of desire, a symbolic overcoding in place of speech, and a fictitious subject of enunciation in place of the analysand. But most of all it turns all human stories into the story of Oedipus.

Freud's reading of Sophocles' *Oedipus Rex* continues to hold that odd fascination that Freud called the uncanny: It is simultaneously familiar and strange, like the play itself. Freud begins by announcing that the "chief part in the mental lives of all children who later become psycho-neurotics is played by their parents" (SE, IV: 260). But he goes on to say that he is convinced that psycho-neurotics are not unique in loving one parent and hating the other, for in this respect they do not differ significantly from "normal" human beings (261). Indeed, it is because Sophocles' tragedy consists entirely of the process of revealing the truth about Oedipus – that he is the murderer of King Laius, that he is Laius' son, and that he has married his mother, Jocasta – it is because it reveals these truths that have been hidden, that its processes "can be likened to the work of a psychoanalysis" (262). The action of the play, then, both captures the universal Oedipal story – that every child loves one parent and hates the other – and anticipates the profession of psychoanalysis, which will make it possible to decode or overcode everyone's story as that of Oedipus. In their reversal of Freud's reading, Deleuze and Guattari argue that rather than exposing the otherwise repressed desire, the Oedipal law that one must not kill one's father and marry one's mother actually "prohibits something that is perfectly fictitious in the order of desire" and persuades those who are subject to the law that they had such a fictional intention. "No," Deleuze and Guattari conclude, "Oedipus is not a state of desire and the drives, it is an *idea*, nothing but an idea that repression inspires in us concerning desire; not even a compromise, but an idea in the service of repression, its propaganda, or its propagation."[17]

As Deleuze and Guattari see it, psychoanalysis has attached itself to a single, repressive myth of the family and has unwittingly allied itself with the kind of family violence that produces schizophrenic breakdowns. They therefore turn, approvingly though selectively, to the work of R. D. Laing and David Cooper, whose clinical experience parallels Guattari's. Like Laing, Deleuze and Guattari see all human beings – whether sane or psychotic – as necessarily split in several ways: in relation to their world, in relation to themselves, as minds tenuously linked to bodies, and as multiple selves. In his book The *Divided Self* (1968), Laing set out to describe the continuum that reaches from the sane condition of the schizoid to the psychotic life of the schizophrenic, while giving compassionate attention to the schizophrenic. A year later Laing delivered the Massey Lectures for the Canadian Broadcasting Company, later published under the title *The Politics of the Family* (1969), There he traced the paths of schizophrenics back to what he alternately calls the "dramatic structure" or the "politics" of the family. Usually, the dramatic structure of a family is unknown to those who live and perpetuate it. What usually sustains families, Laing argues, is a collective fantasy of the family that all its members share and to which they feel they should sacrifice themselves. To grow up in such families, where we are ignorant even of our ignorance, is to learn the parts we are expected to play, both in the family drama and in life outside the family. These parts or roles may come to constitute a false-self system, analogous to the repertoire of an actor in a touring company. The greatest danger in this dramatic structure of the family is that the self of the actor never develops, that it atrophies, or that it is undermined in various ways. Then, when a given role (parent or child, wife or husband, teacher or student) can no longer be played and the false-self system begins to collapse, there may be no inner self capable of reassembling the shattered life. Here, to continue the analogy with drama, the vulnerability of King Lear replaces the initial confidence of Oedipus. In such situations as this, psychiatry and psychoanalysis scandalously have rushed to the support of the family rather than the schizophrenic. Indeed, it may be, Laing observes, that given a particular family fantasy, the breakdown of the schizophrenic is what is truly authentic, while the family's politics is violent. Perhaps we sometimes misconstrue a breakthrough as a breakdown.

Deleuze and Guattari approvingly construct a useful pastiche of quotations from Laing's *The Politics of Experience* (1967) in an effort to show the similarities among his work, theirs, and Foucault's studies in madness:

If the human race survives, future men will, I suspect, look back on our enlightened epoch as a veritable age of Darkness. They will presumably be able to savor the irony of this situation with more amusement than we can extract from it. The laugh's on us. They will see that what we call "schizophrenia" was one of the forms in which, often through quite ordinary people, the light began to break through the cracks in our all-too-closed minds. . . . Madness need not be all breakdown. It may also be breakthrough . . . The person going through ego-loss or transcendental experiences may or may not become in different ways confused. Then he might legitimately be regarded as mad. But to be mad is not necessarily to be ill, notwithstanding that in our culture the two categories have become confused . . . From the alienated starting point of our pseudo-sanity, everything is equivocal. Our sanity is not "true" sanity. Their madness is not "true" madness. The madness of our patients is an artifact of the destruction wreaked on them by us and by them on themselves. Let no one suppose that we meet "true" madness any more than that we are truly sane. The madness that we encounter in "patients" is a gross travesty, a mockery, a grotesque caricature of what the natural healing of that estranged integration we call sanity might be. True sanity entails in one way or another the dissolution of the normal ego.[18]

Immediately following this quotation, Deleuze and Guattari recall that their visit to London was a visit to Pythia, not just because of Laing's work there at the Tavistock Clinic but because in London they saw the paintings of Turner, particularly those of his final period. In the Venetian paintings "all that remains is a background of gold and fog, intense, intensive, traversed in depth by what has just sundered its breadth: the schiz."[19] In these paintings the breakthrough rather than the breakdown can be witnessed, as it can also, Deleuze believed, in much of Anglo-American literature and in the writings of Kafka and Proust. That Freud attributed the origins of art – as well as religion, morality, and society – to the Oedipus complex (SE, XIII: 156) is but a further indication of his determination to use psychoanalysis to return the ego to its place of supremacy.

Lacan too had strenuously objected to the ego-orientation of psychoanalysis, and his understanding of desire was his most important supplement to Freud's thought. However, for Deleuze and Guattari, Lacan's sense of desire as an unfillable lack that orients both the human subject and language to a future that never arrives is an idealistic, dialectical, nihilistic conception.[20] Although they seem to agree with Lacan that desire shapes the human subject, for them desire is an unbounded force that is natural, social, unconscious, and "irreducible to any sort of unity."[21] It is desire that produces multiplicity.

In their critique of capitalism, Deleuze and Guattari might at first seem more affirmative of Marx than they are of Freud, but this difference is more a matter of tone than substance. Just as they work to free Freud from the confines of the Oedipal family, so also do they rethink Marx in order to libidinalize his understanding of production. Although they do not explicitly cite this example, Deleuze and Guattari find Marx and Engels's conception of the family, like Freud's, monolithic and simplistic. The *Manifesto for the Communist Party*, for example, claims that the family is a bourgeois institution that will "vanish with the vanishing of capital" (SW, 49). In addition to their suspicion of Marx's monolithic explanations, the two most important corrections to Marx that Deleuze and Guattari offer are their objections to his distinction between production, distribution, exchange, and consumption and to his related distinction between use value and exchange value. These distinctions are fundamental to Marx's project because they are the basis of his claim that social relations are determined by economic ones. What Deleuze and Guattari object to here is that Marx's analysis, powerful as it is, has not gone far enough.

The exchange value of an object is determined by Marx in relation to other commodities – for example, the value of a generic brand of canned corn in relation to a brand name of canned corn – while the use value is determined in relation to human needs – for example, the value of a snow shovel in July in relation to its value in December. What Marx leaves insufficiently explored, however, is the dynamics of need or lack. This may be because his Darwinian materialism predisposes him to think of need as a given consequence of the dialectics of nature (SW, 338). Deleuze and Guattari point out that far from being natural, need or lack is a production of a dominant class that has the power to manipulate market economy. Thus, wants and needs are deliberately organized "amid an abundance of production, making all of desire teeter and fall victim to the great fear of not having one's needs satisfied."[22] Deleuze and Guattari insist that "Everything is production, *production of productions*, of actions and of passions; *productions of recording processes*, of distributions and of co-ordinates that serve as points of reference; *productions of consumptions*, of sensual pleasures, of anxieties, and of pain."[23] It is therefore necessary to couple desiring and production together and to think of them as one concept. Perhaps the most surprising feature of Deleuze and Guattari's argument in *Anti-Oedipus* is that they link psychoanalysis to capitalism rather than to Marxism. Their project – unlike Erich Fromm's, for example – is not to bring Freud and Marx into some sort of comfortable alliance. On the contrary, what they see is that "the discovery of an activity of production *in general and without distinction*, as it appears in capitalism is the identical discovery of *both* political economy *and* psychoanalysis."[24]

The last book Deleuze and Guattari wrote together was entitled *What Is*

Philosophy? (1991), a question, they claim, that can only be asked late in life when one has reached a point of nonstyle that allows one to ask, in effect, what one has done all one's life.[25] Unlike the final works of Titian, Turner, Monet, Chateaubriand, and Kant (all of whom they mention), this is a book of quiet simplicity. It is a book that wants to be elegant rather than profound, perhaps because it is not a book of philosophy but instead a book about doing philosophy. "Philosophy," they argue, "is the art of forming, inventing, and fabricating concepts," or, at least, that is what philosophy has become.[26] Concepts, however, do not exist alone. They require "conceptual personae" who play a part in their definition. One of the earliest of these personae – in Plato, for example – is the friend, which provides a vivid reminder that thought involves relationship to an Other, a point that may be in danger of being lost in contemporary analytical philosophy. Philosophy, then, is not mere contemplation, reflection, or communication; rather it is the creation of signed concepts in relationship to others. Furthermore, these concepts, although they are named and dated, "have their own way of not dying" (8), so long as they are being renewed by criticism and mutation. This final point puts the critical procedures of *Anti-Oedipus* into a new and somewhat brighter light. Far from being an effort to destroy or supersede the thought of Freud and Marx, Deleuze and Guattari's critique gives it new life by turning its best insights back upon itself, by pushing it further than it had the courage to go, and by bringing it forward into the present.

Foucault's assessment of Deleuze's work has veen often cited: "Perhaps one day, this century will be known as Deleuzian."[27] Far more than a tribute to a colleague and friend with whom he sometimes disagreed even to the point of estrangement, Foucault's assessment might simply be read as a straightforward description of the range of Deleuze's accomplishments: He was the best critical historian (or genealogist) of philosophy in postwar France. He read the texts of Marx and Freud to a critical standard set by Althusser and Lacan. He espoused the coherence of Nietzsche's thought in a way that influenced an entire generation of French intellectuals. He anticipated some of the most important insights of Foucault and Derrida. He was a brilliant theorist of cinema and painting. But he was also a committed teacher and political activist, not last but first. For students of literature, Deleuze also left the challenge to ask of a text not " 'What does it mean?' but rather 'How does it work?' "[28] That is, he was exceptionally sensitive to the dangers of interpretive methods, whether Freudian, Marxist, or Deleuzian. What particularly engaged him was what he called "schizo-analysis," which is an effort to recognize how certain texts promote new modes of knowledge, how they produce the creative divisions of the unconscious, and how they foster the dynamic multiplicity of the human subject. Such texts always subvert every effort to contain them. For example, much as he was drawn to Shakespeare and Sophocles, Freud neither countered Bottom's dismissal of dream interpretation – "a man is but an ass if he go about to expound this dream" – nor did he heed Jocasta's ironically appropriate dismissal of her husband-son's dawning realization of the truth about himself when she says (perhaps in a tone of boredom): "many a man hath dreamt as much."

NOTES

1 *Dialogues*, trans. Hugh Tomlinson and Barbara Habberjam (New York: Columbia University Press, 1987), p. vii.
2 *Dialogues*, pp. 51–2.
3 A coinage, apparently, by Ronald Bogue in his excellent book *Deleuze and Guattari* (London: Routledge, 1989), p. 9.
4 *Dialogues*, p. 52.
5 *Anti-Oedipus: Capitalism and Schizophrenia*, trans. Robert Hurley, Mark Seem, and Helen R. Lane (Minneapolis: University of Minnesota Press, 1983), p. 1.
6 *Anti-Oedipus*, p. 7.
7 Michel Foucault, "Theatrum Philosophicum," in *Language, Counter-Memory, Practice*, trans. Donald F. Bouchard and Sherry Simon (Ithaca, NY: Cornell University Press, 1977), p. 165.
8 "Theatricum Philosophicum," p. 167.
9 *Dialogues*, p. 18.
10 *Nietzsche and Philosophy*, trans. Hugh Tomlinson (New York: Columbia University Press, 1983), pp. 2–3.
11 *Dialogues*, p. 77.
12 Ibid., p. 78.
13 Ibid.
14 Ibid., pp. 78–9.
15 Ibid., p. 79.
16 Ibid., p. 80.
17 *Anti-Oedipus*, pp. 114–15.
18 Quoted in *Anti-Oedipus*, pp. 131–2, from R. D. Laing, *The Politics of Experience* (New York: Ballantine Books, 1967), pp. 129, 133, 138, 144.
19 *Anti-Oedipus*, p. 132.
20 Ibid., p. 25.
21 Ibid., p. 42.
22 Ibid., p. 28.
23 Ibid., p. 4.
24 Ibid., p. 302.

25 *What Is Philosophy?* trans. Hugh Tomlinson and Graham Burchill (London: Verso, 1994), p. 1.

26 Ibid., p. 2.

27 "Theatrum Philosophicum," p. 165.

28 *Anti-Oedipus*, p. 109.

Index